ACTIVE HANDS

ACTIVITY BOOKS 4-6 | VOL -1 | HOW TO DRAW

ActivityCrusades

Published by Speedy Publishing Canada Limited

ActivityCrusades
activity books

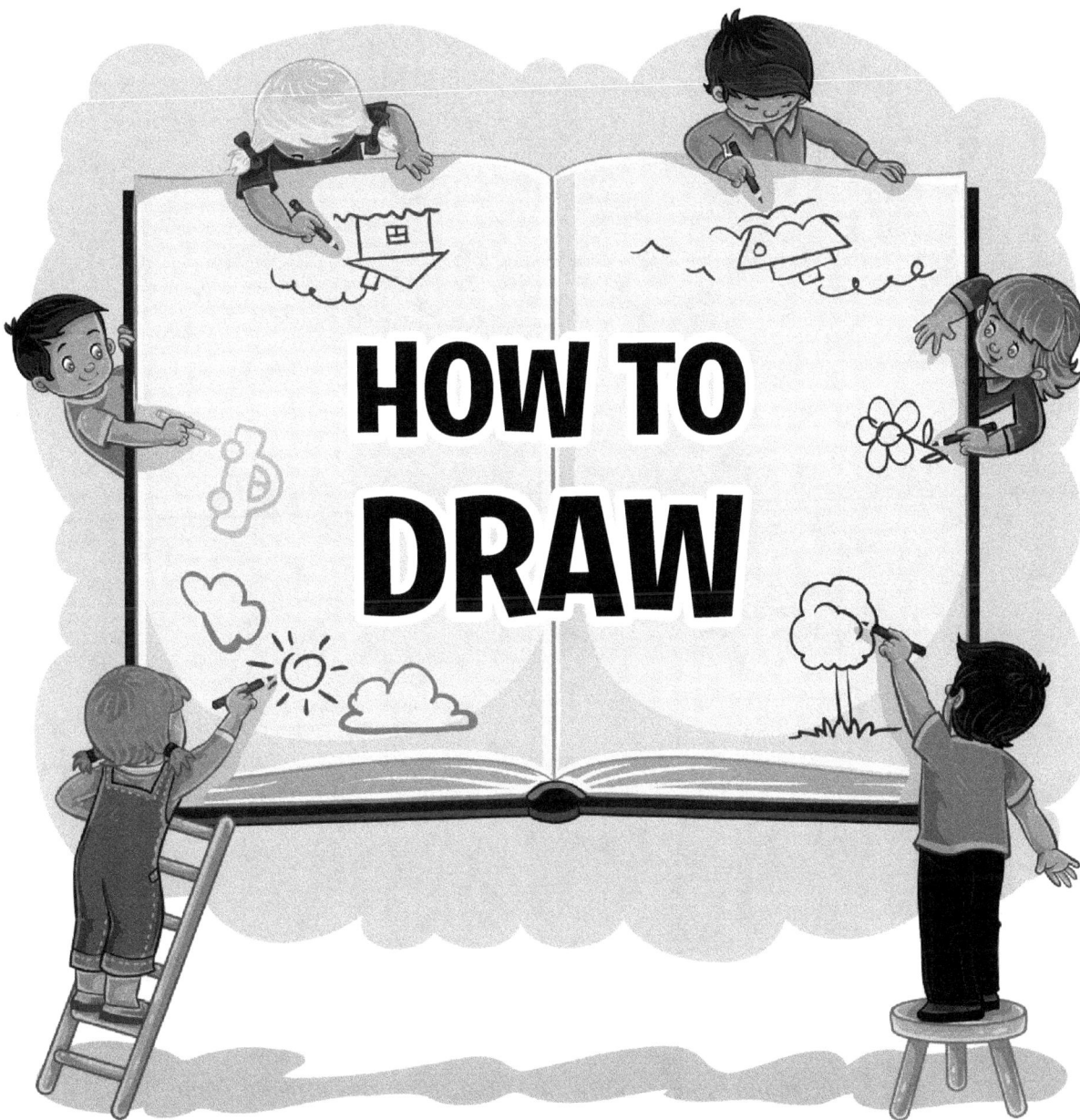

HOW TO DRAW

CAN YOU COPY THIS?

Draw the image with the lines
as your guide then color it!

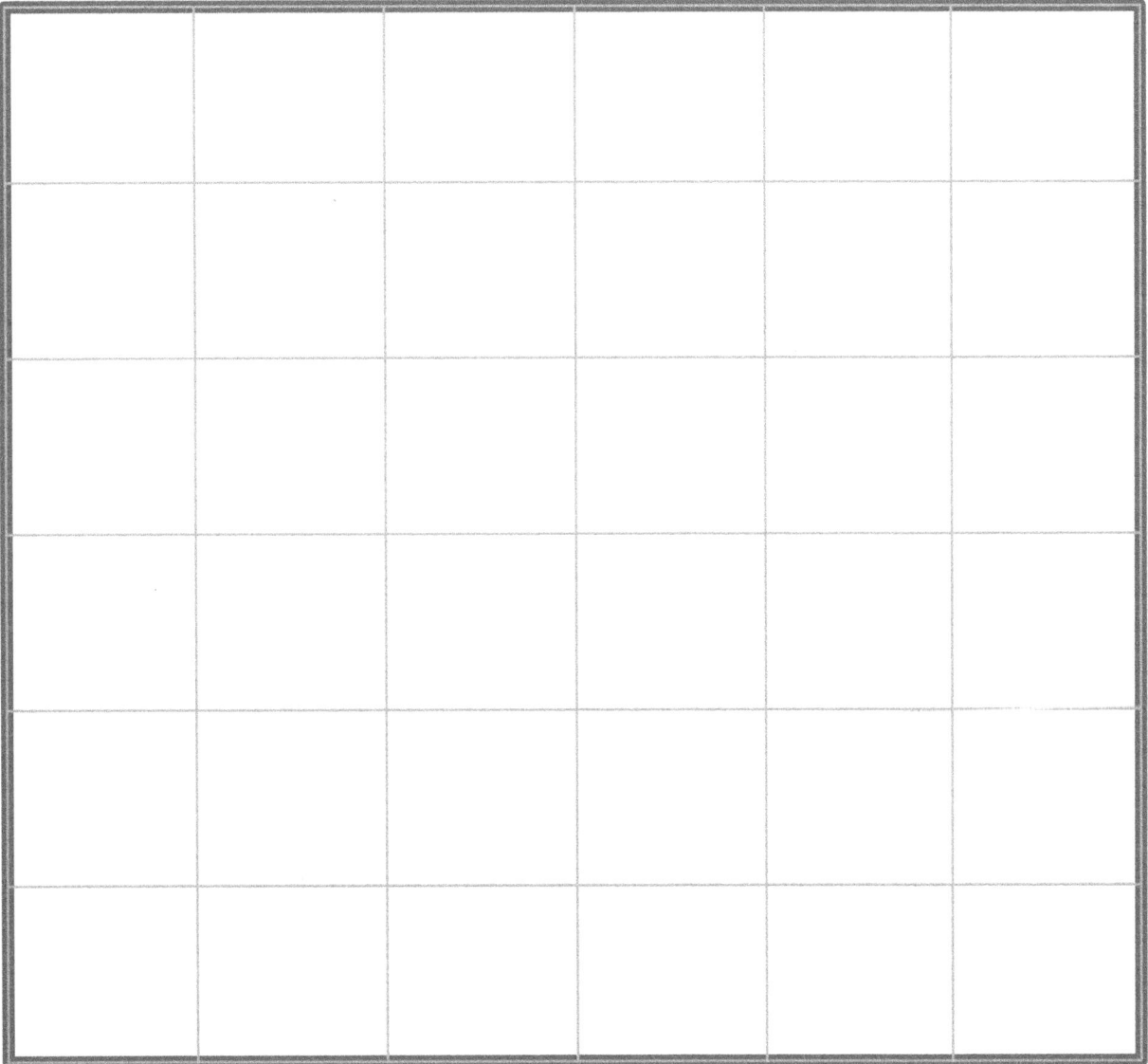

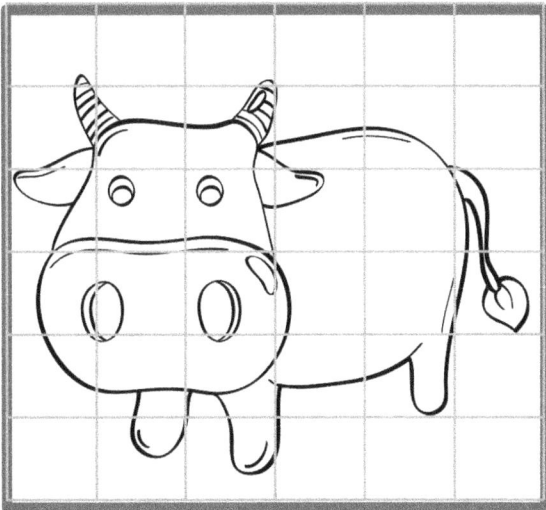

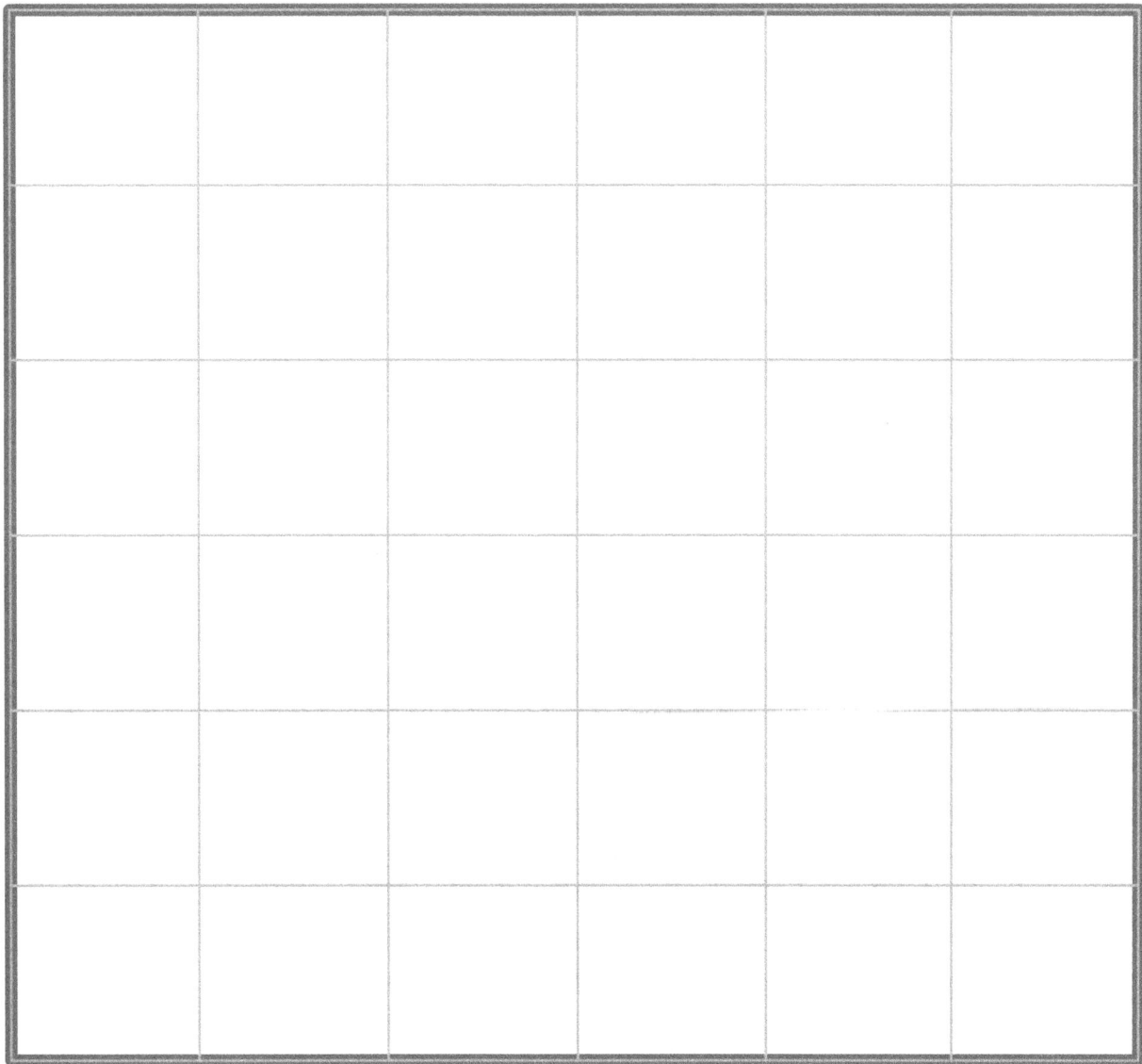

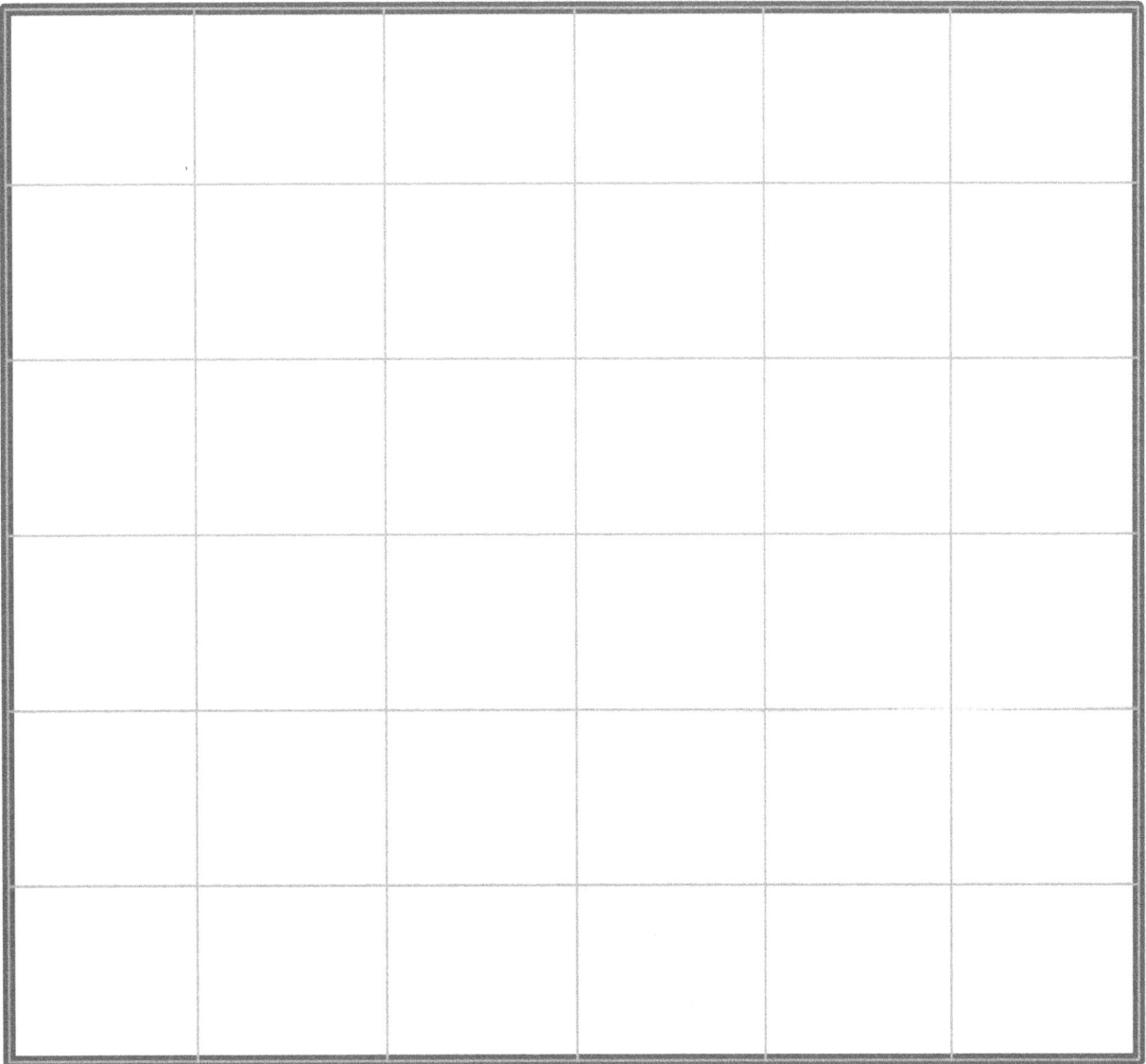

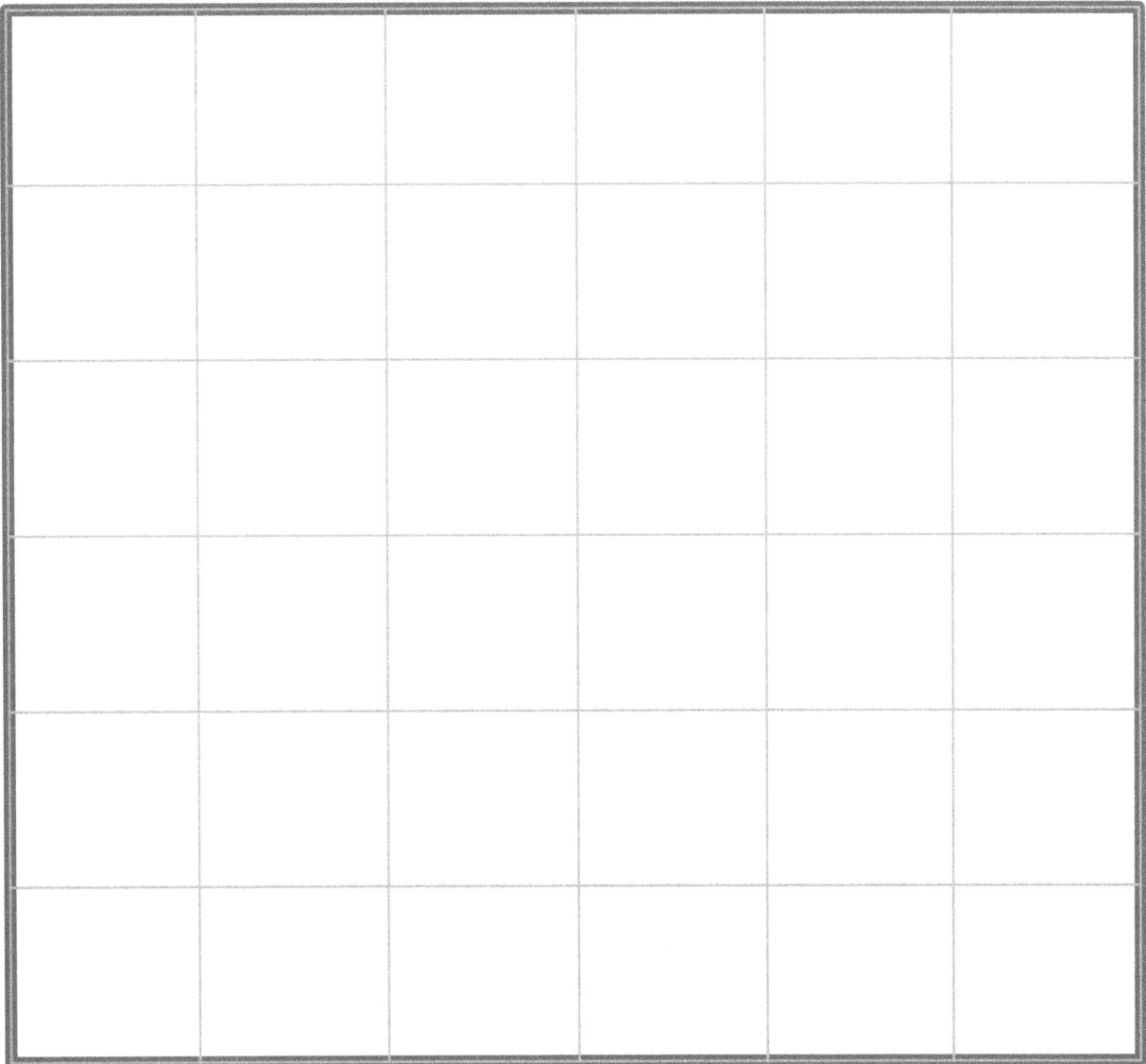

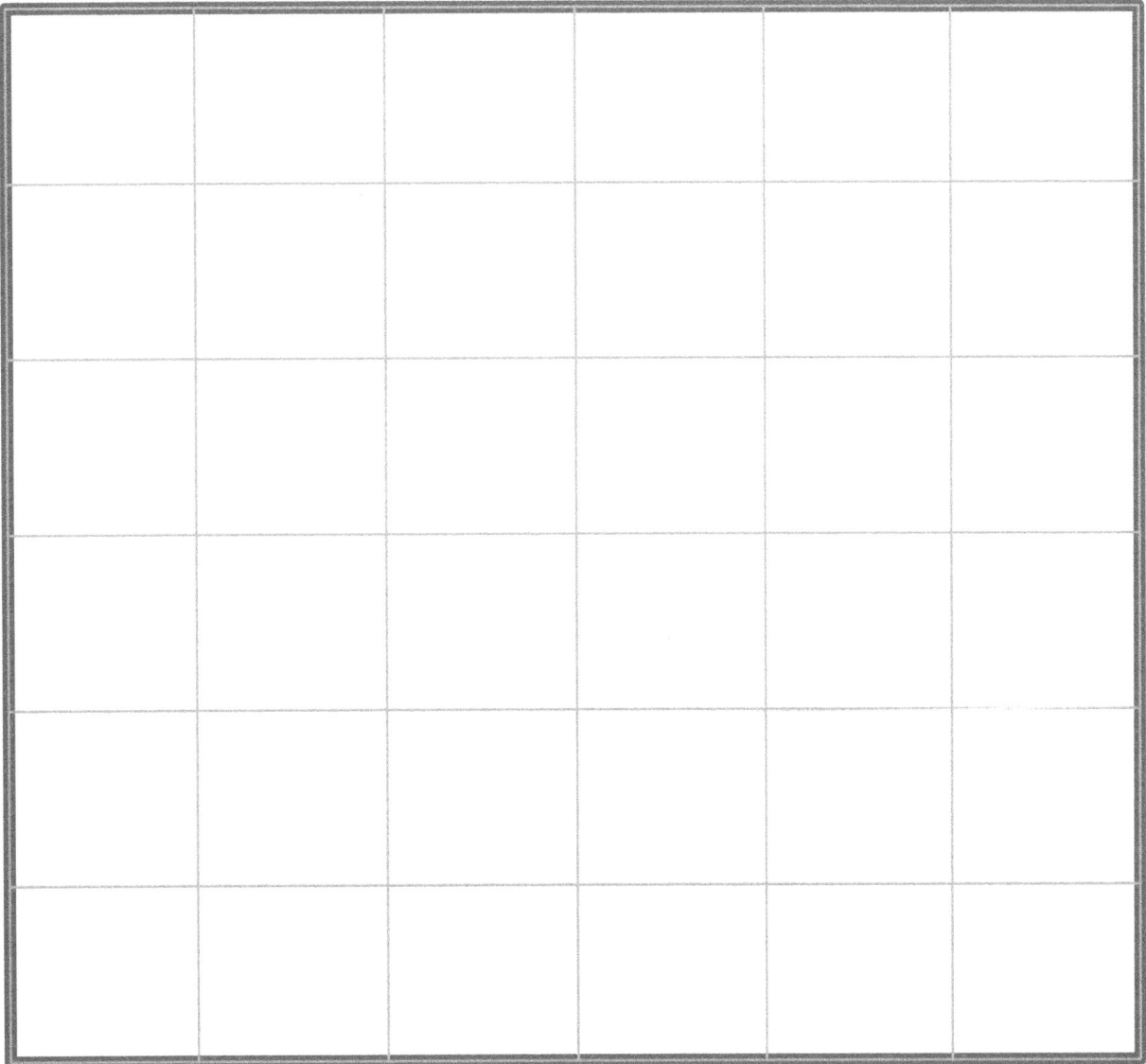

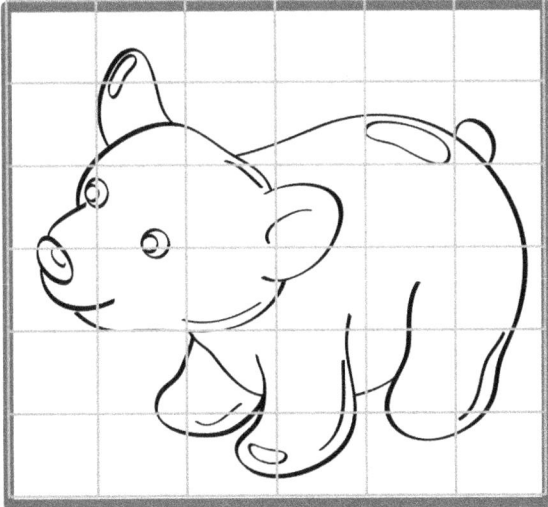

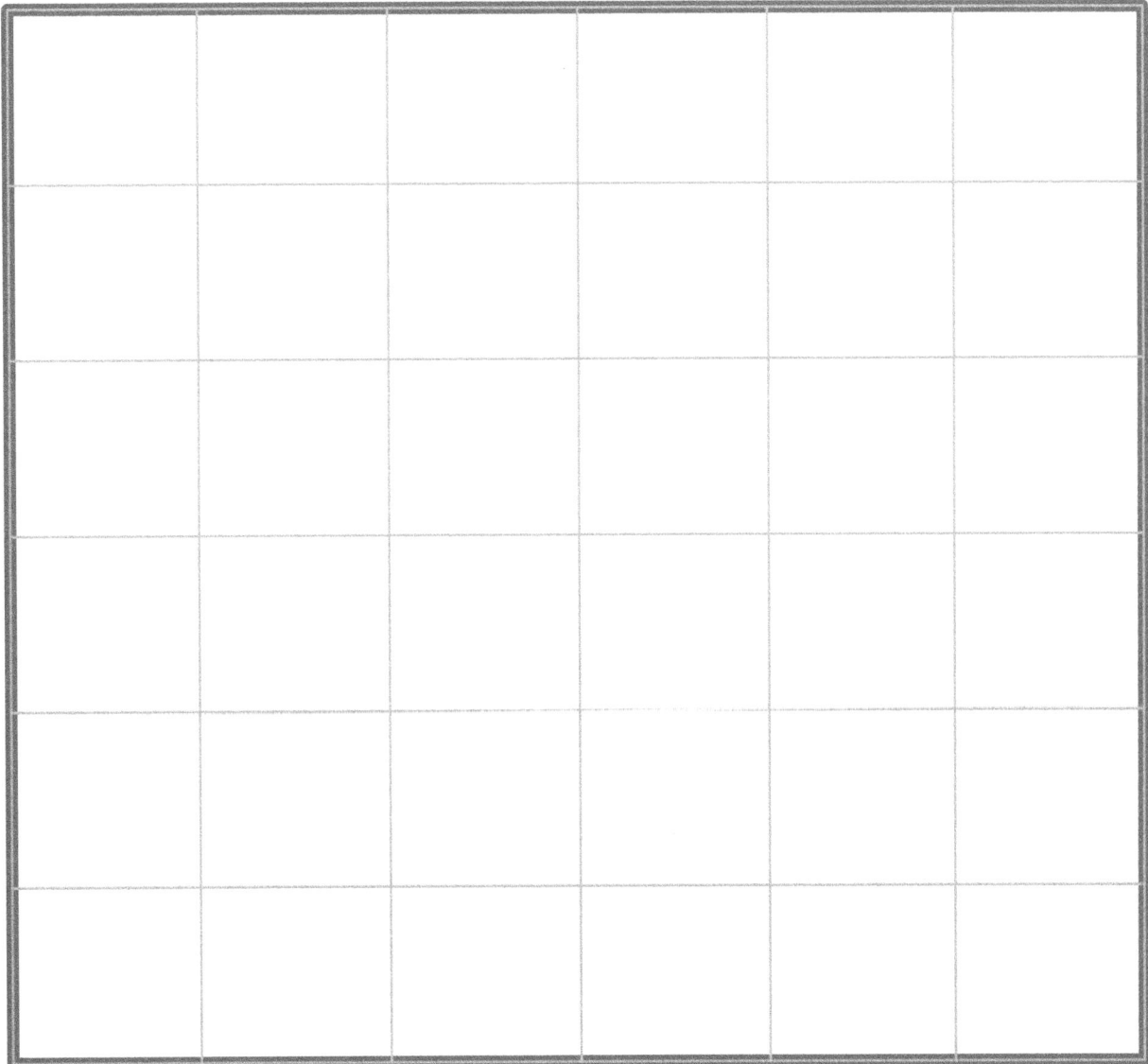

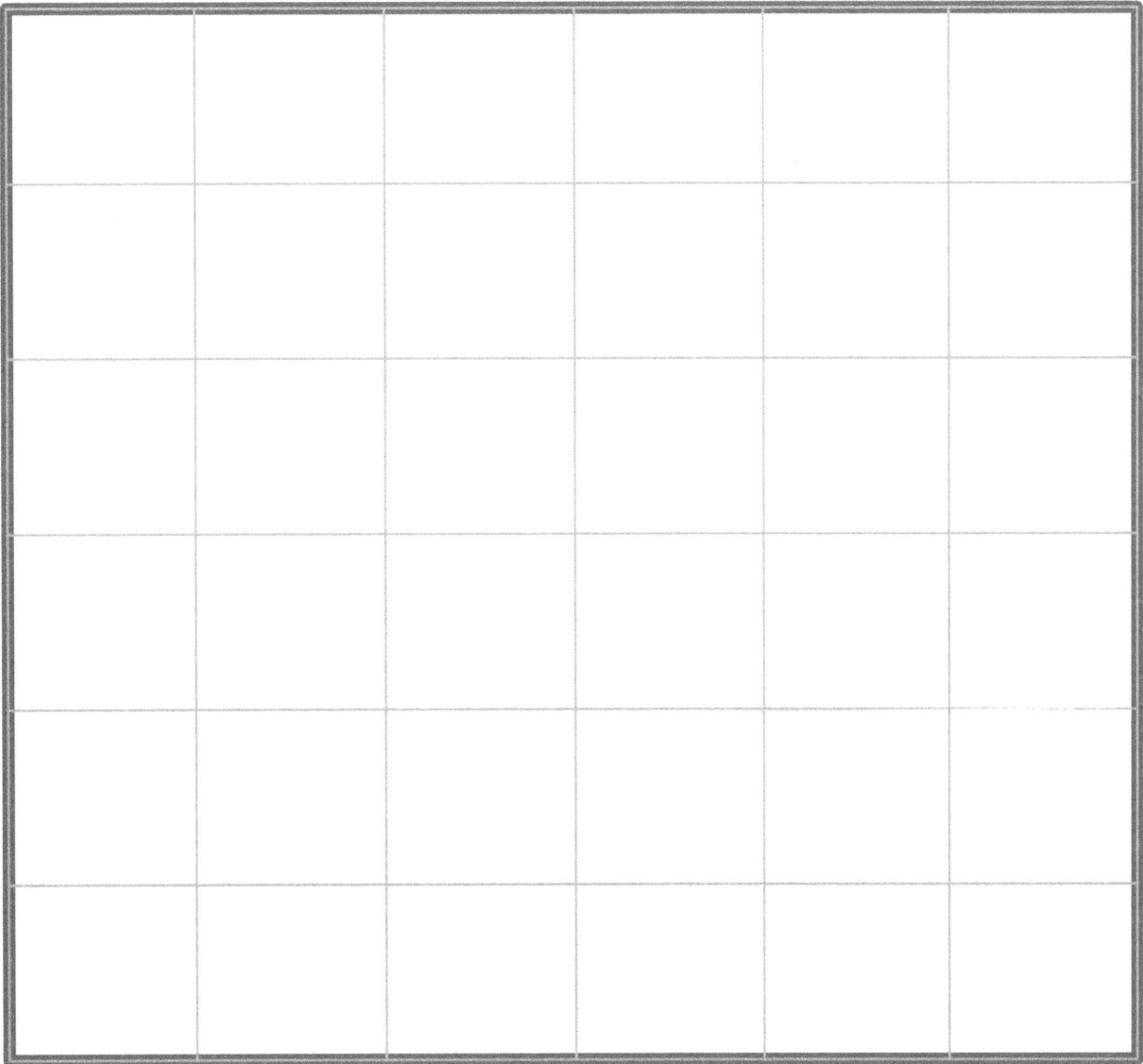

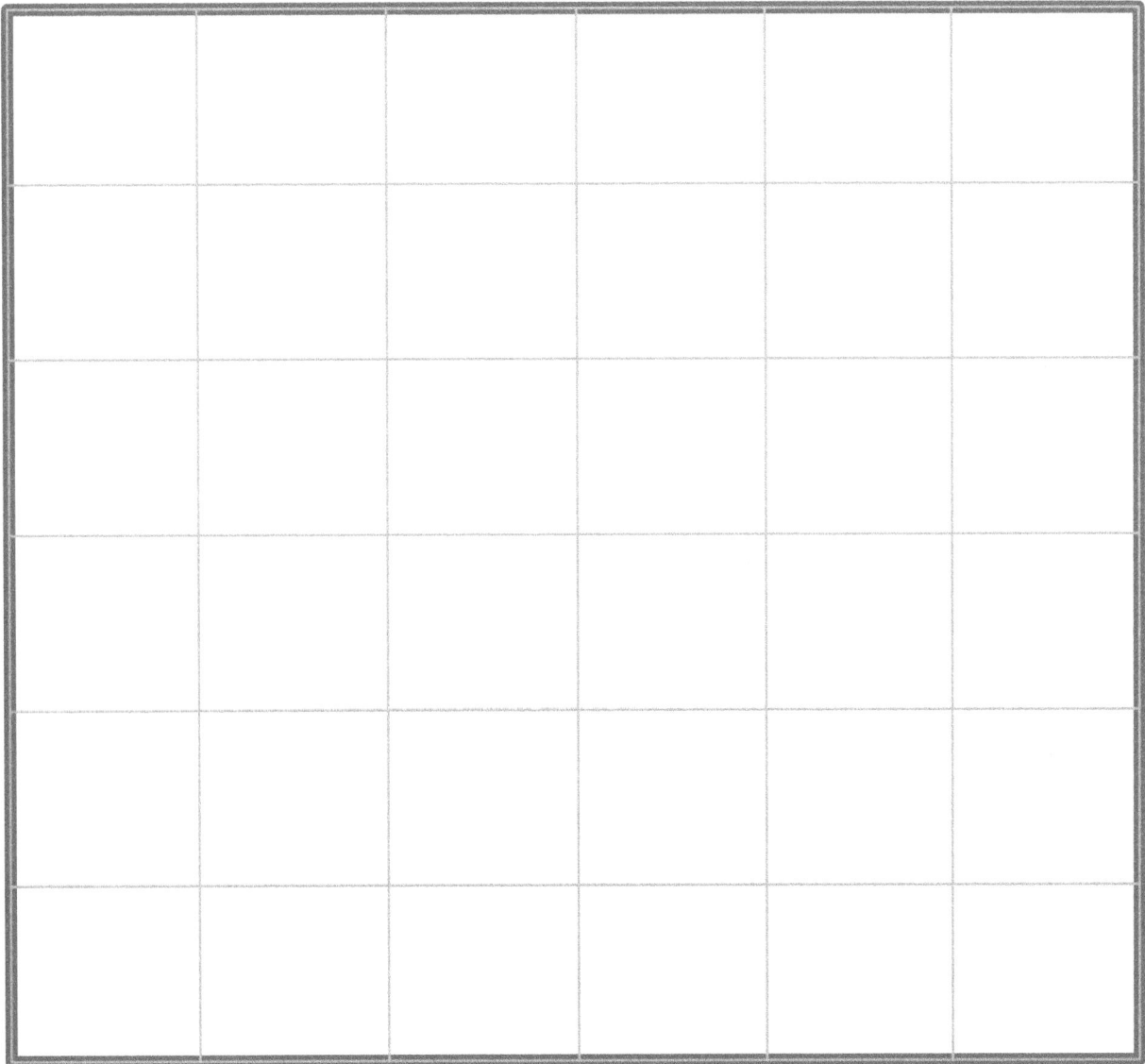

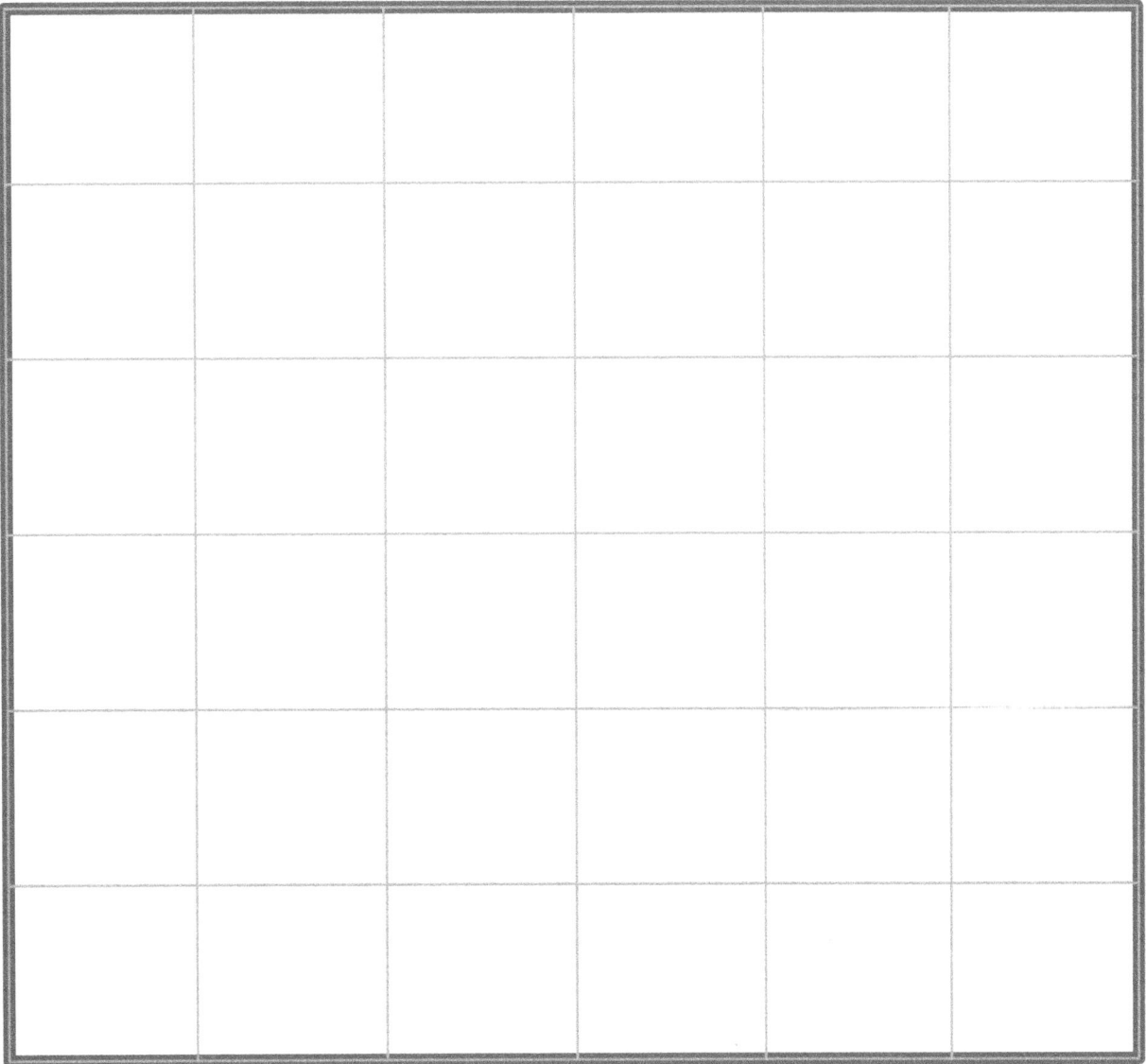

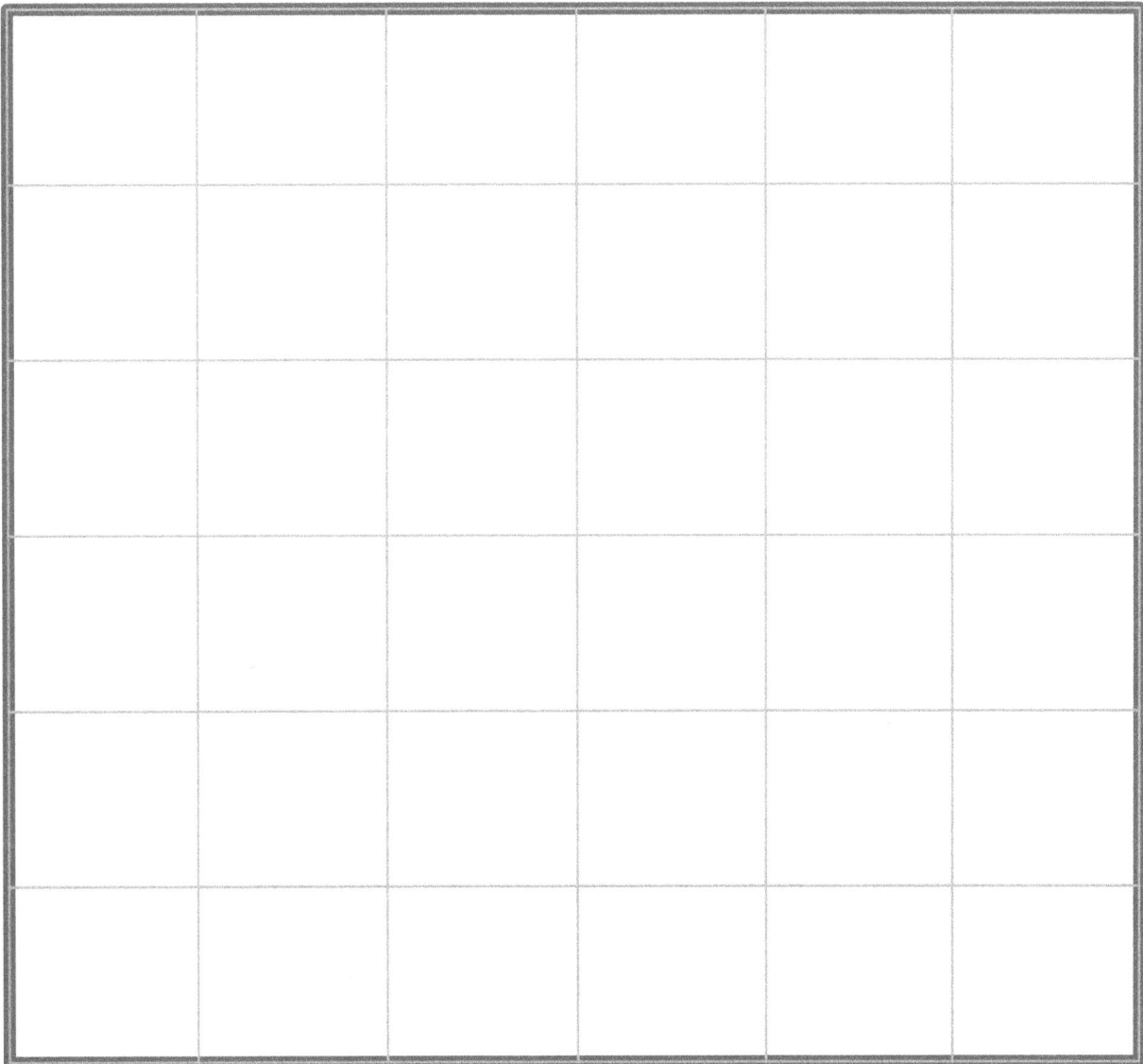

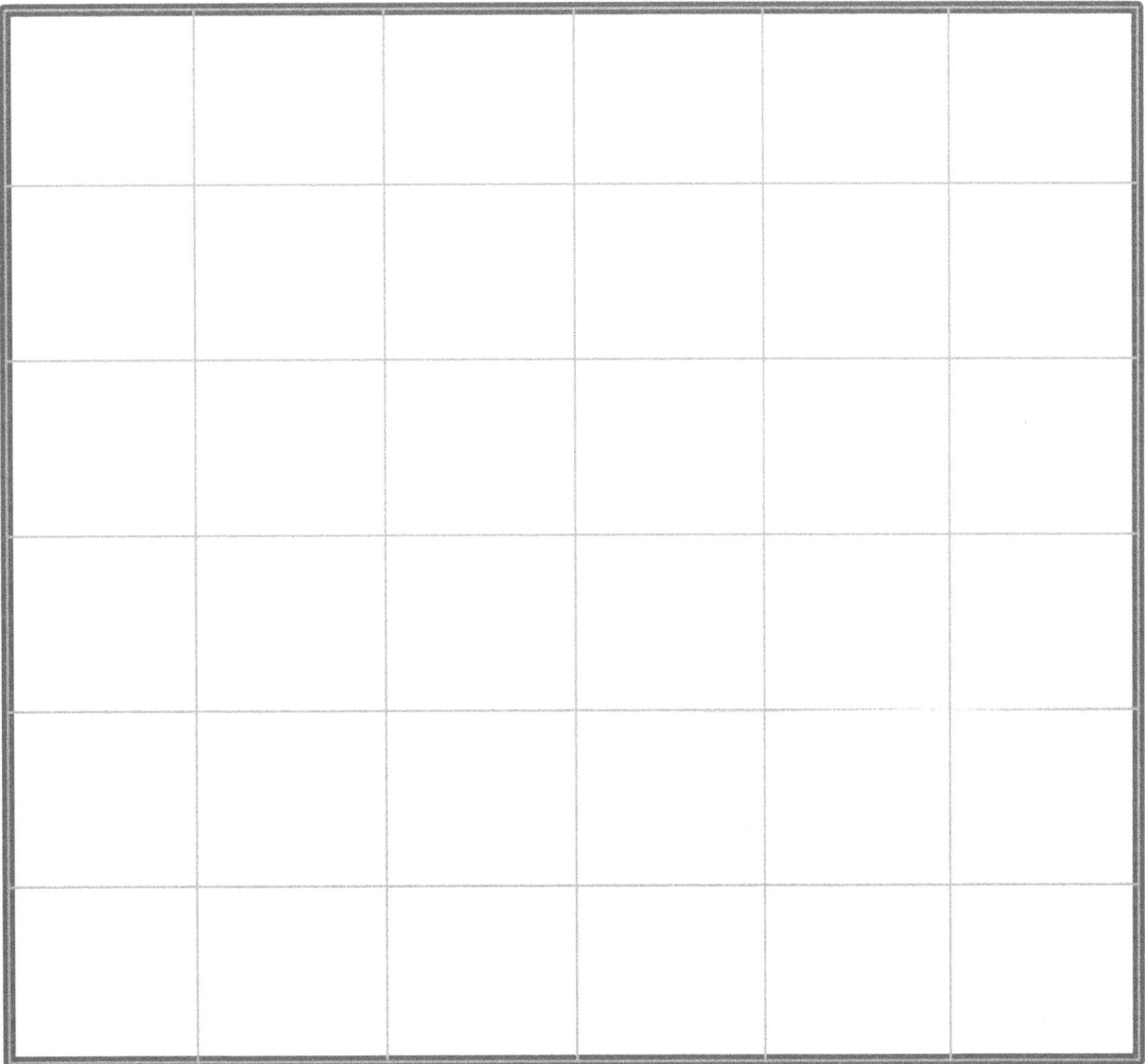

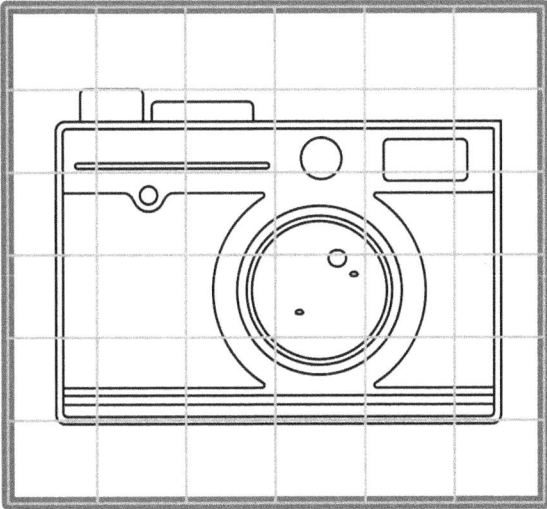

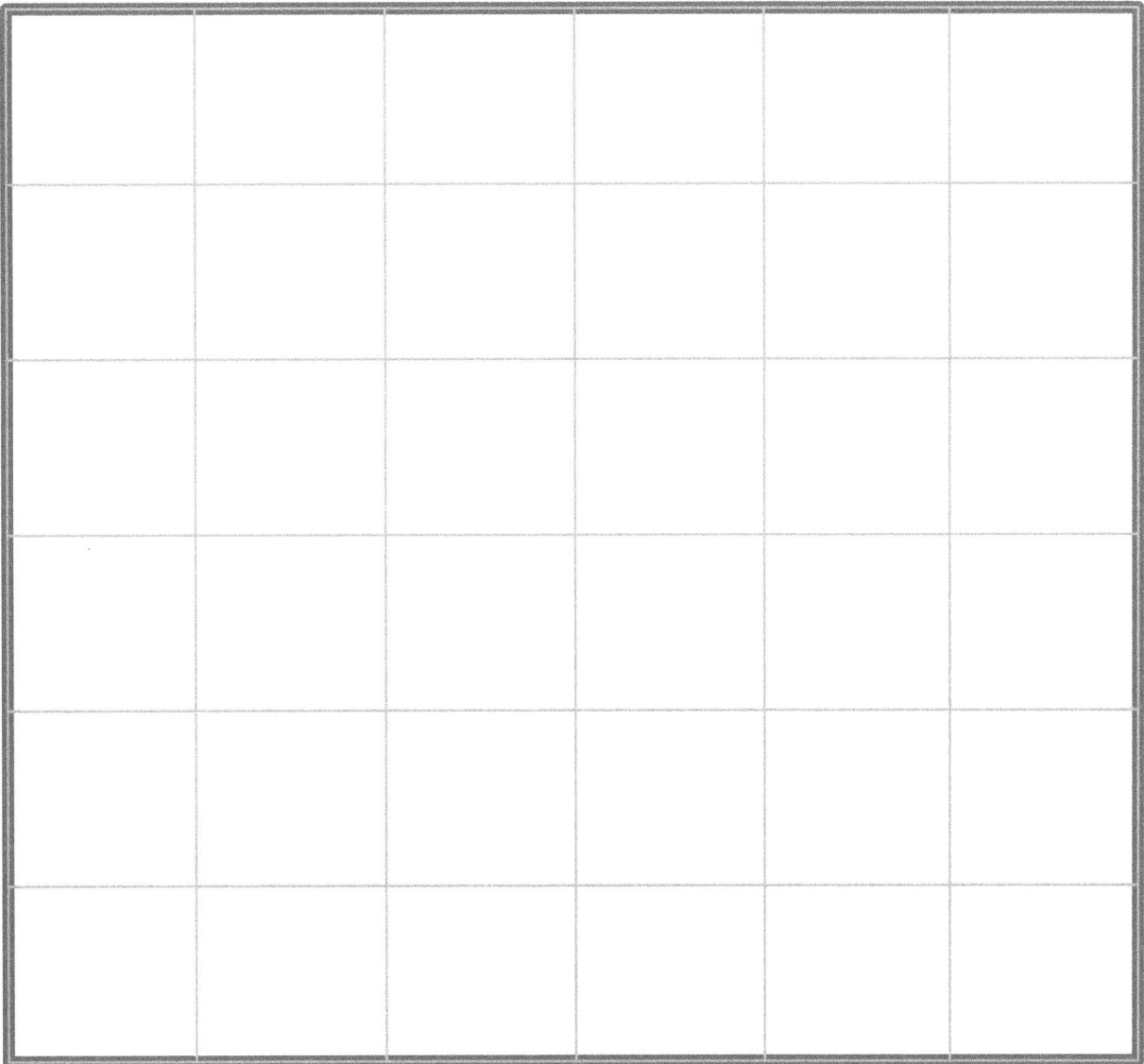

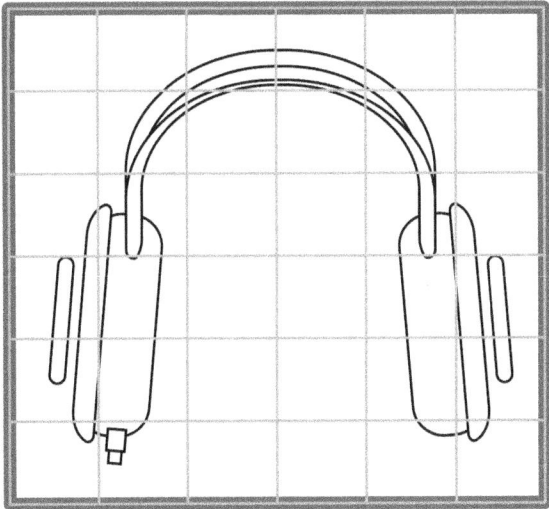

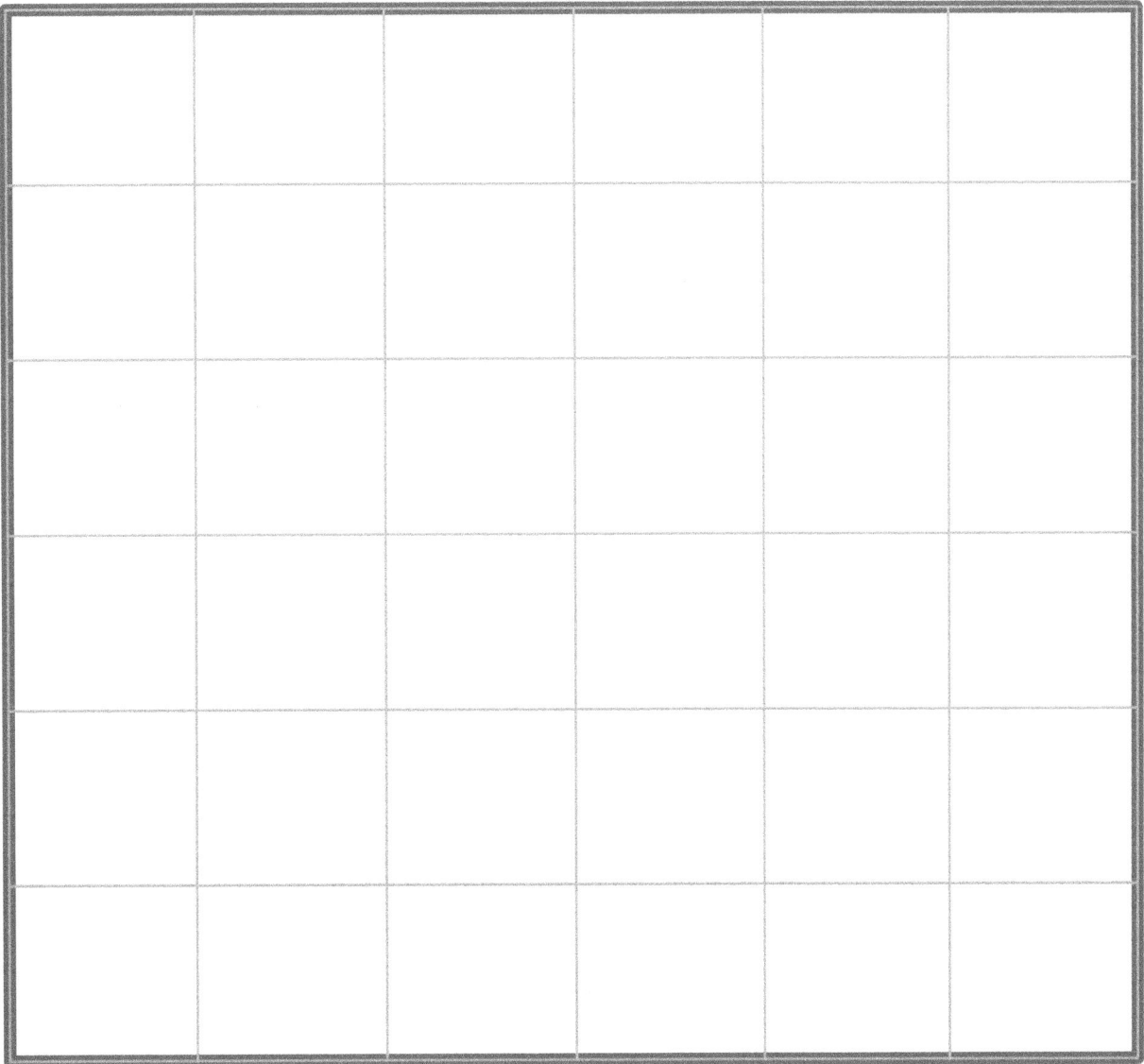

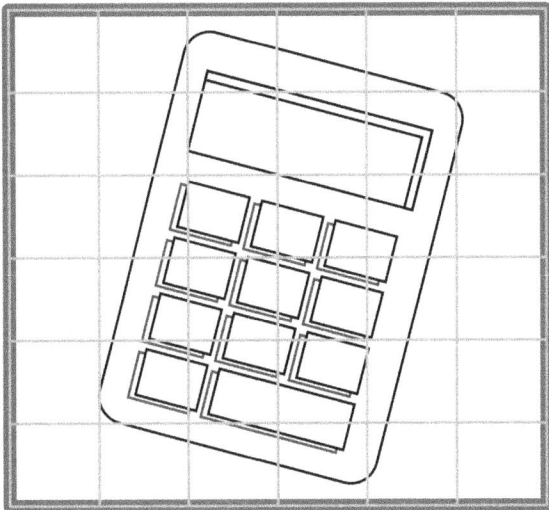

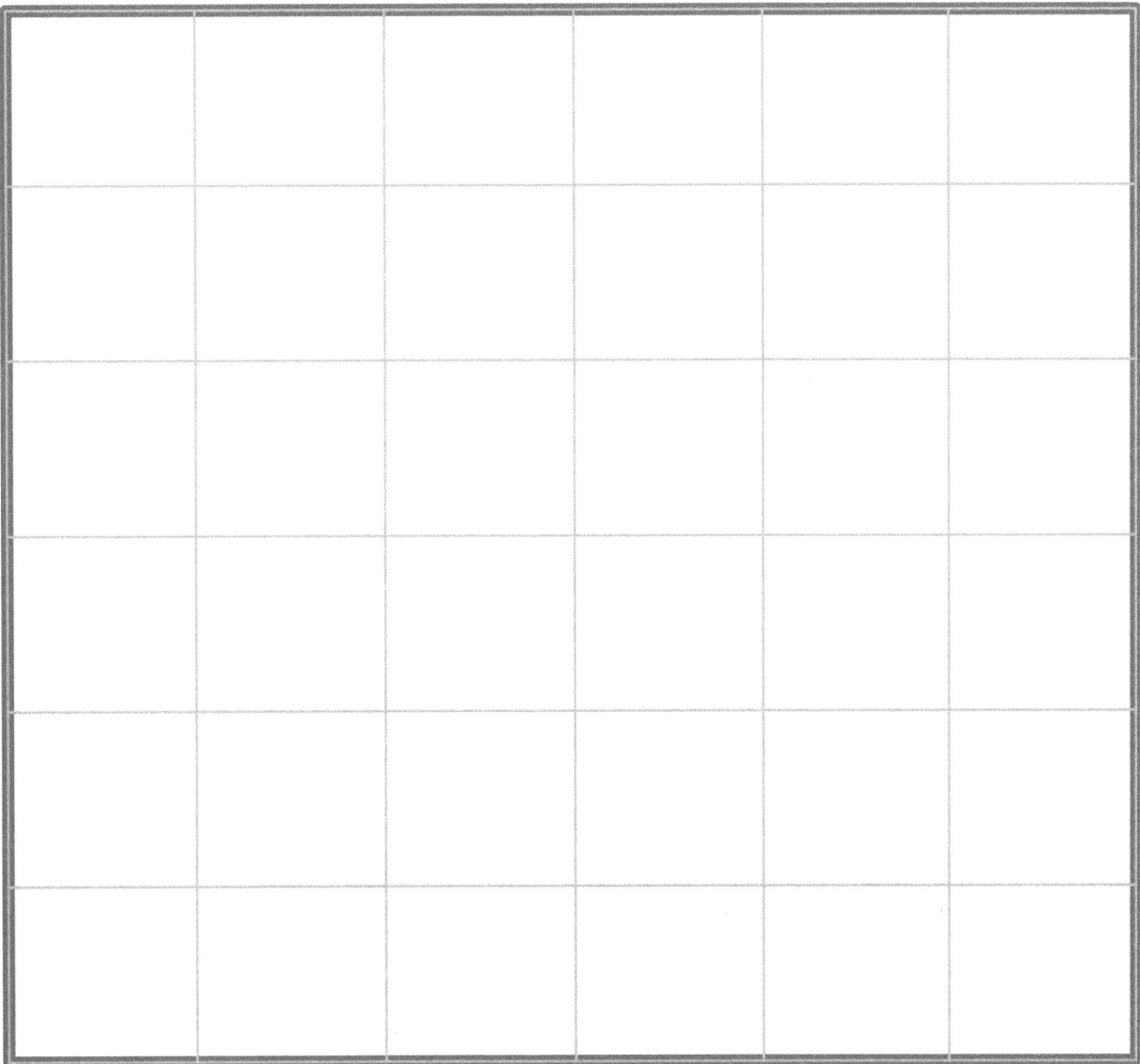

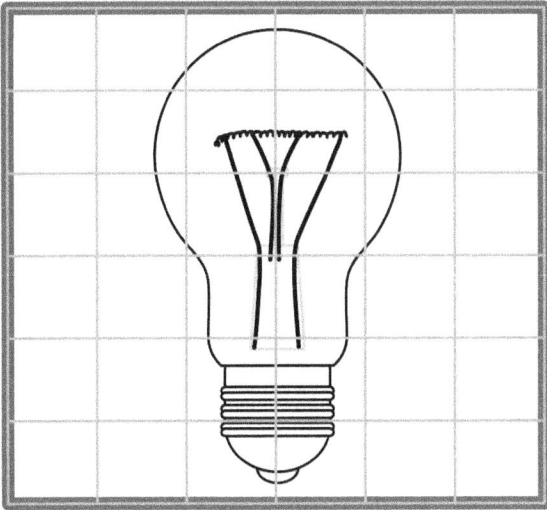

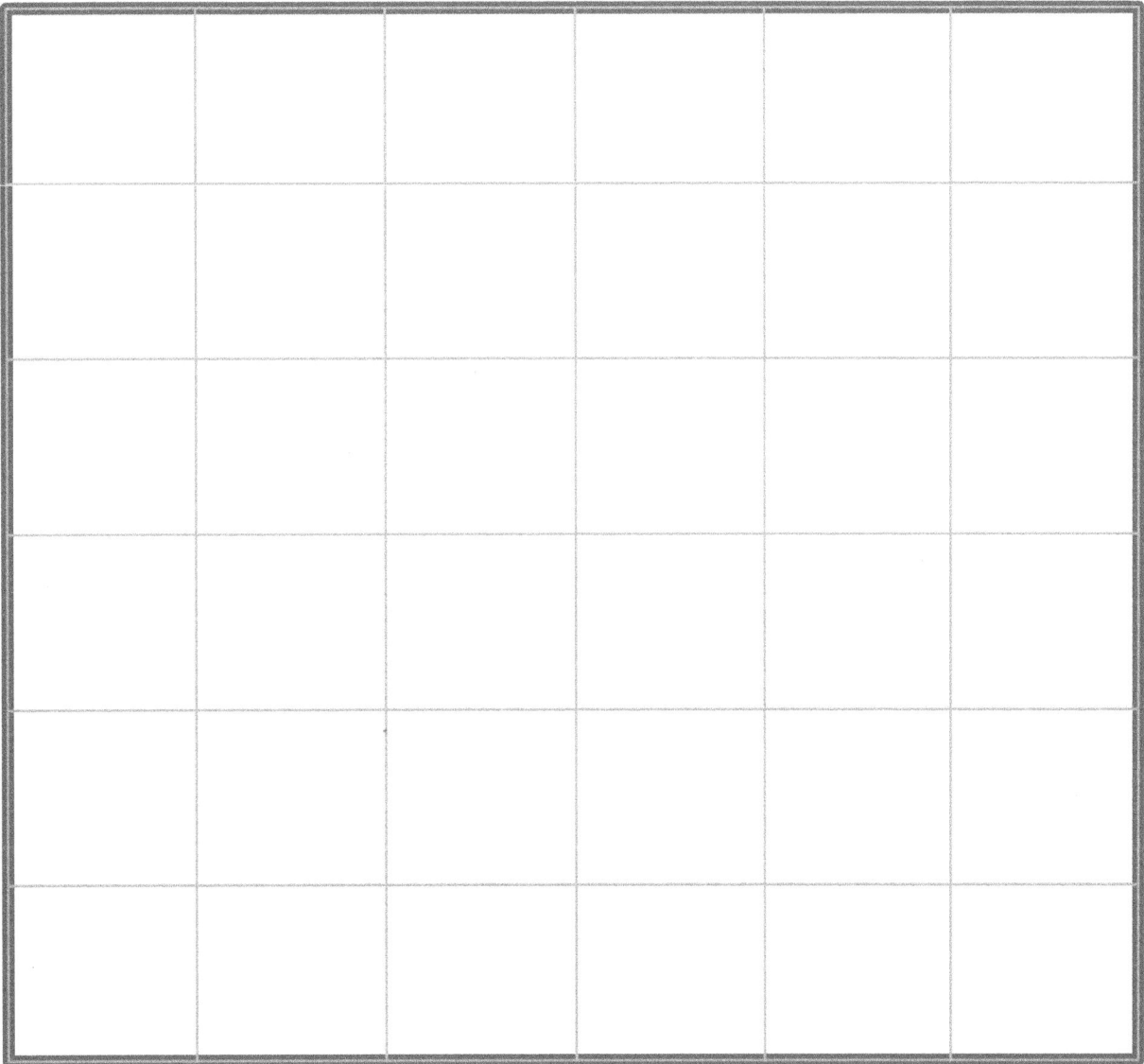

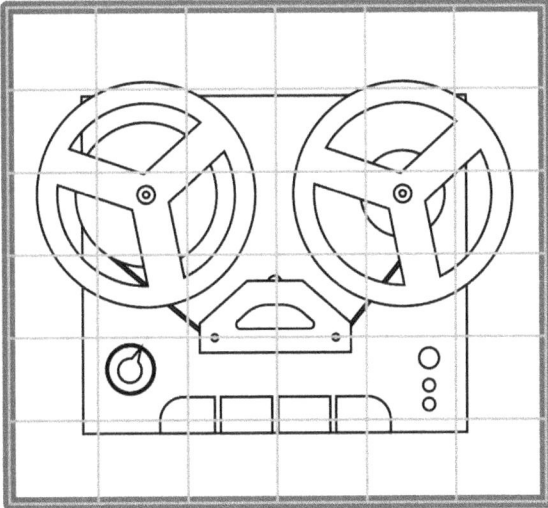

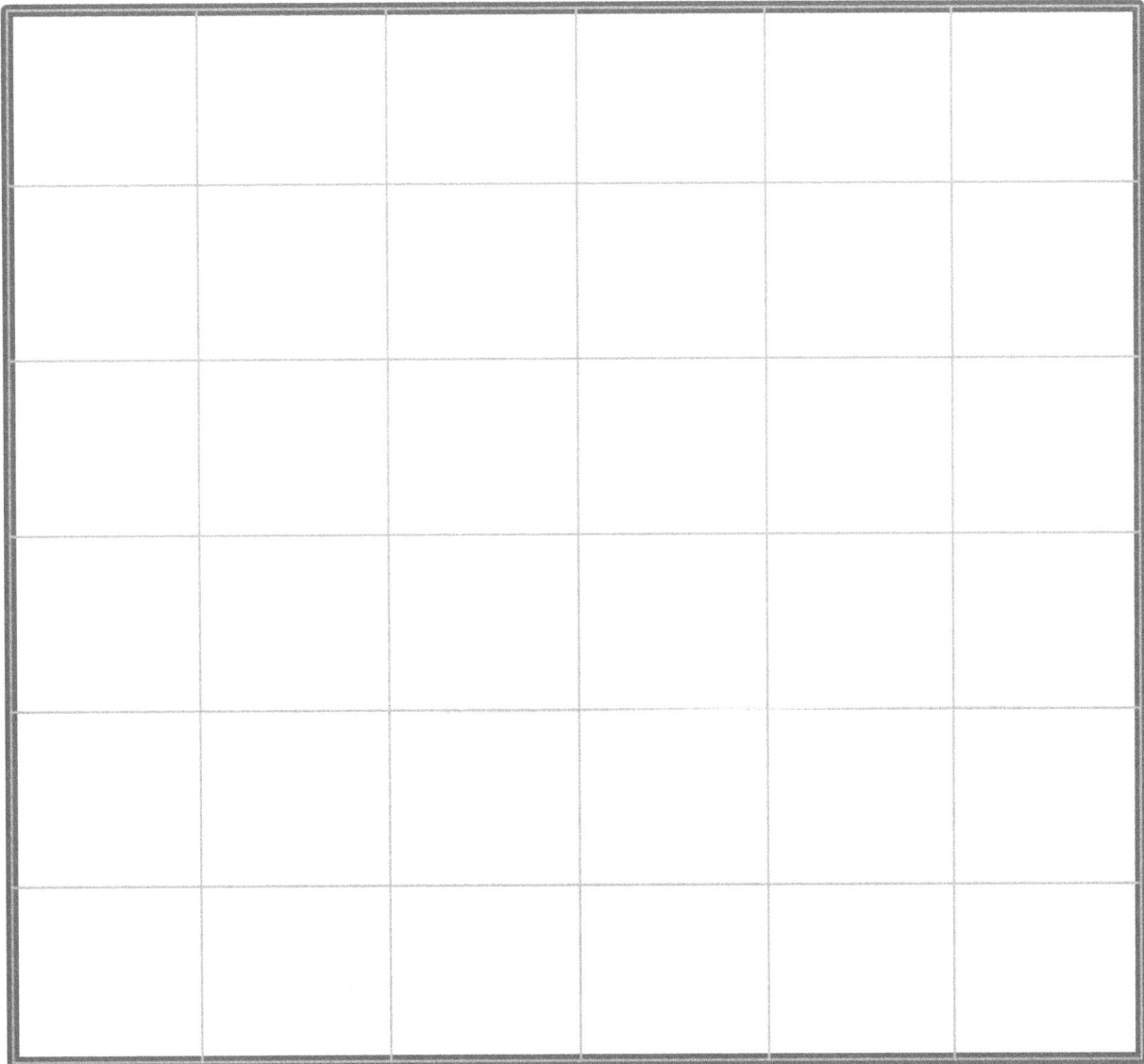

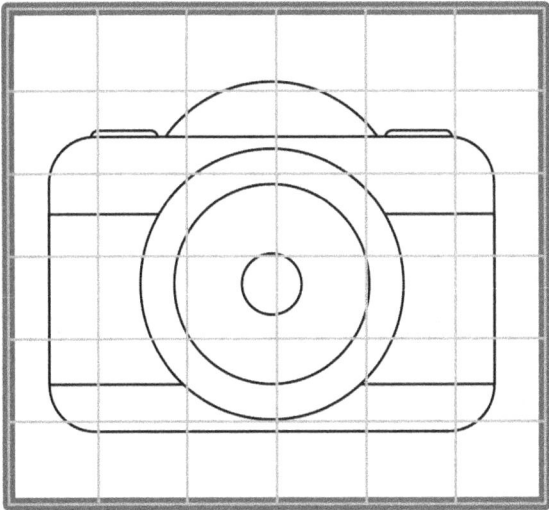

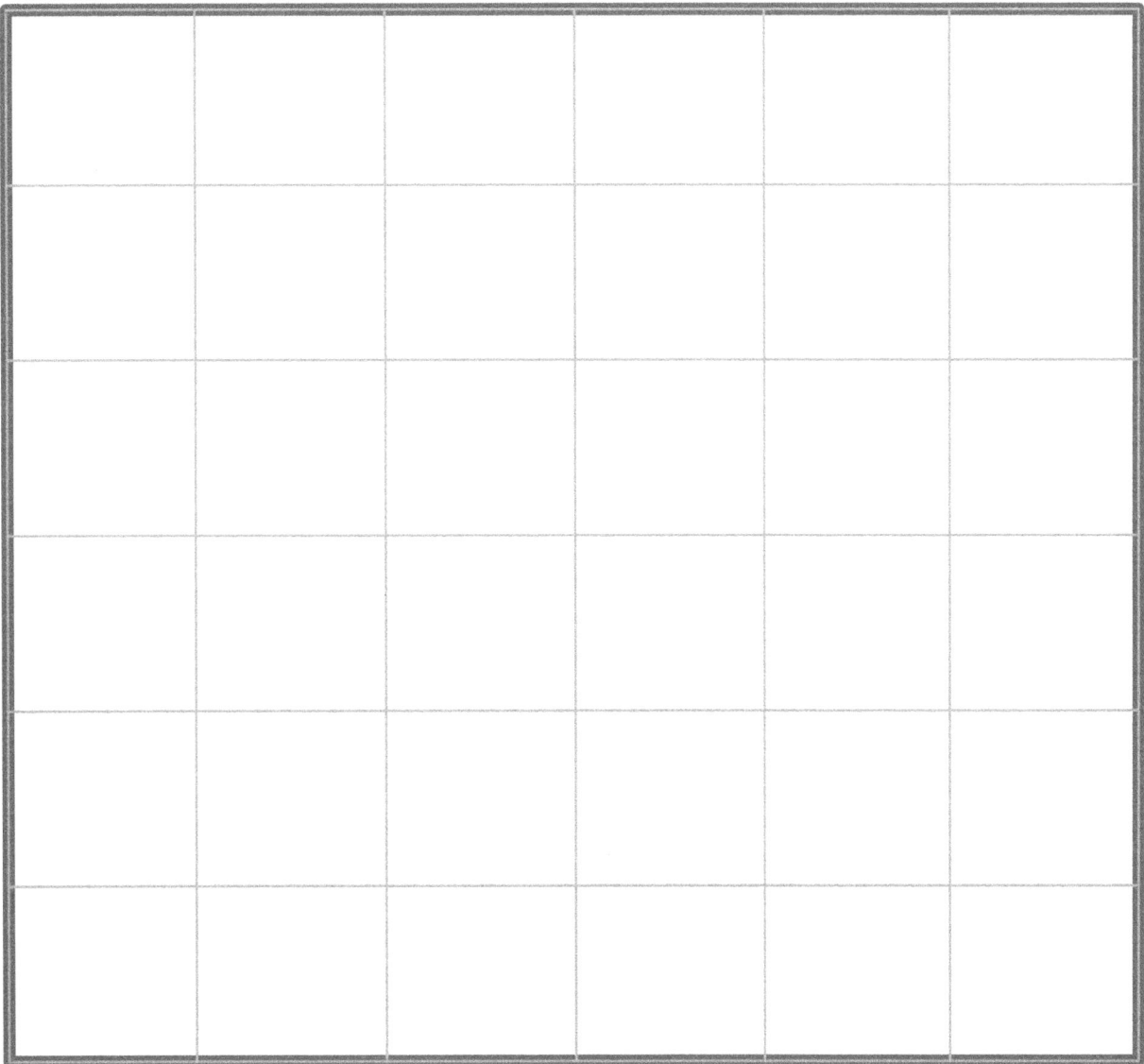

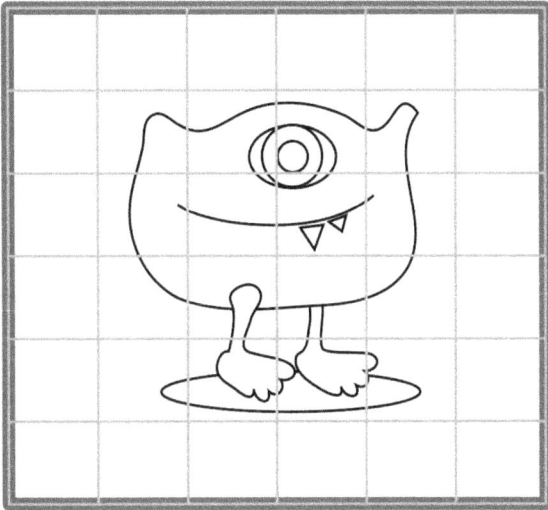

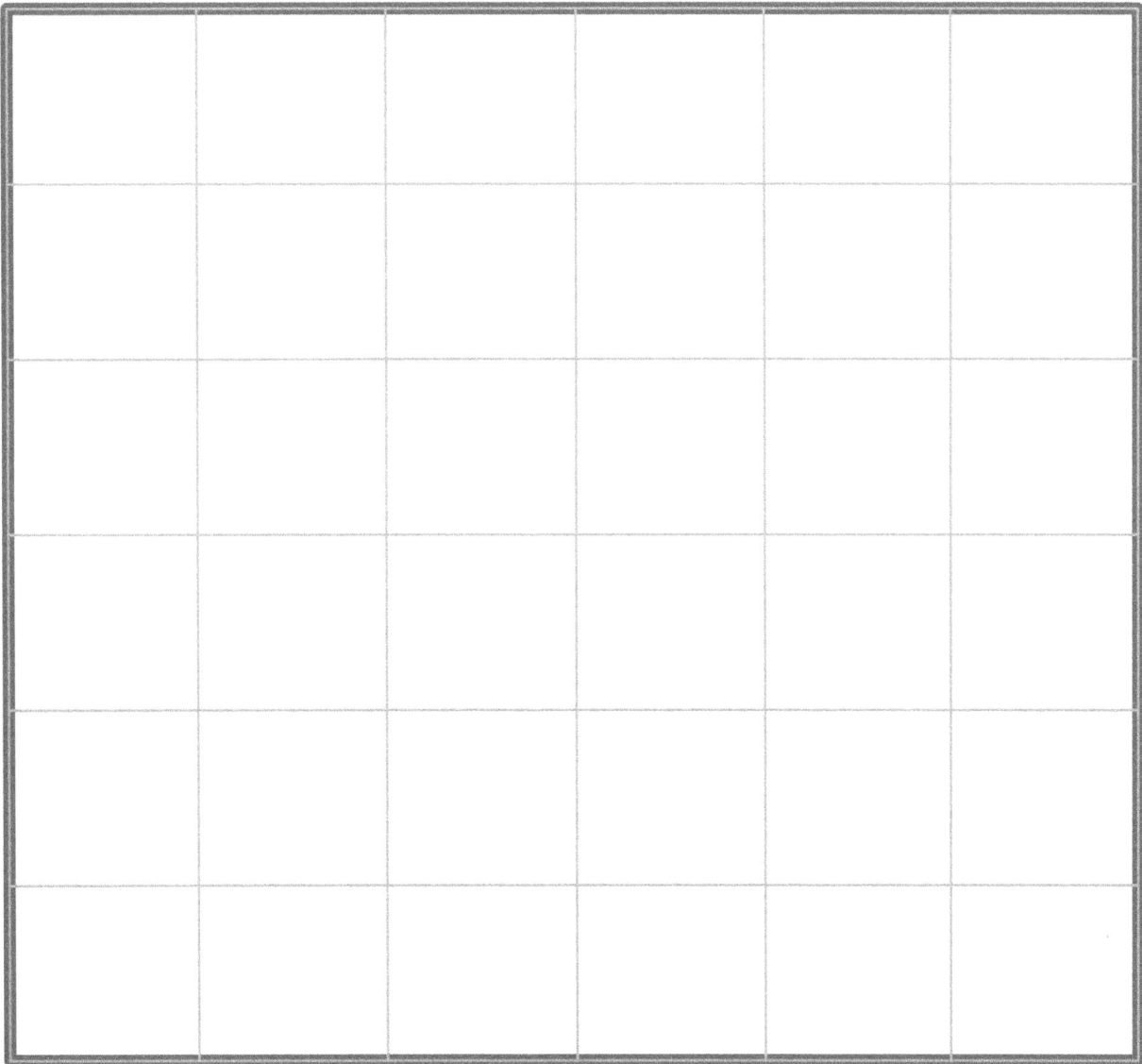

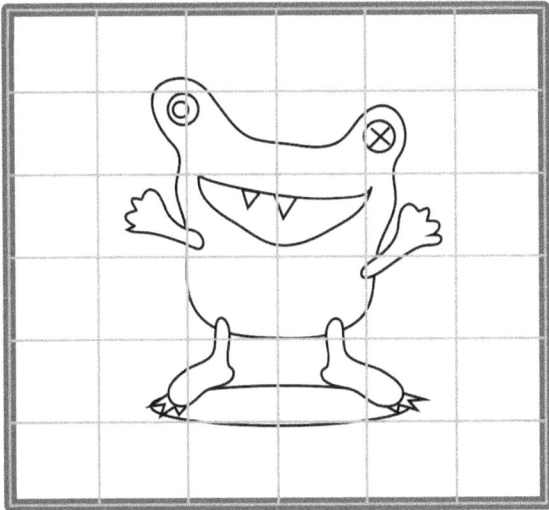

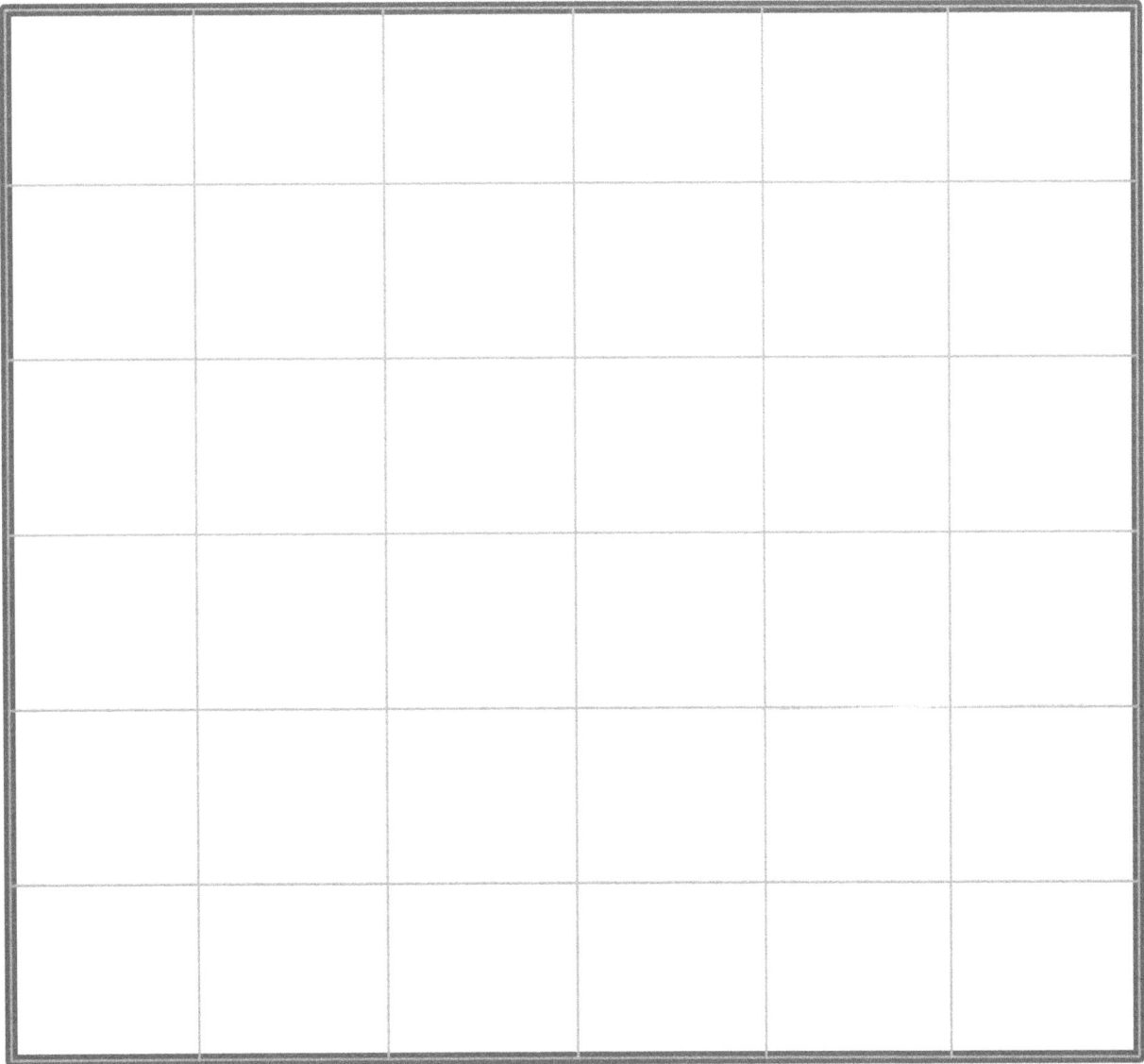

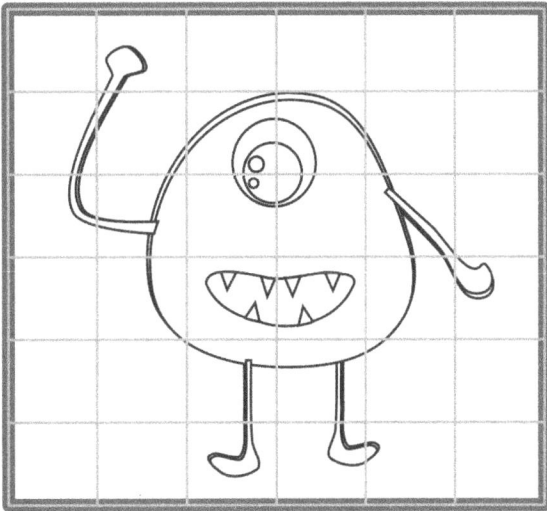

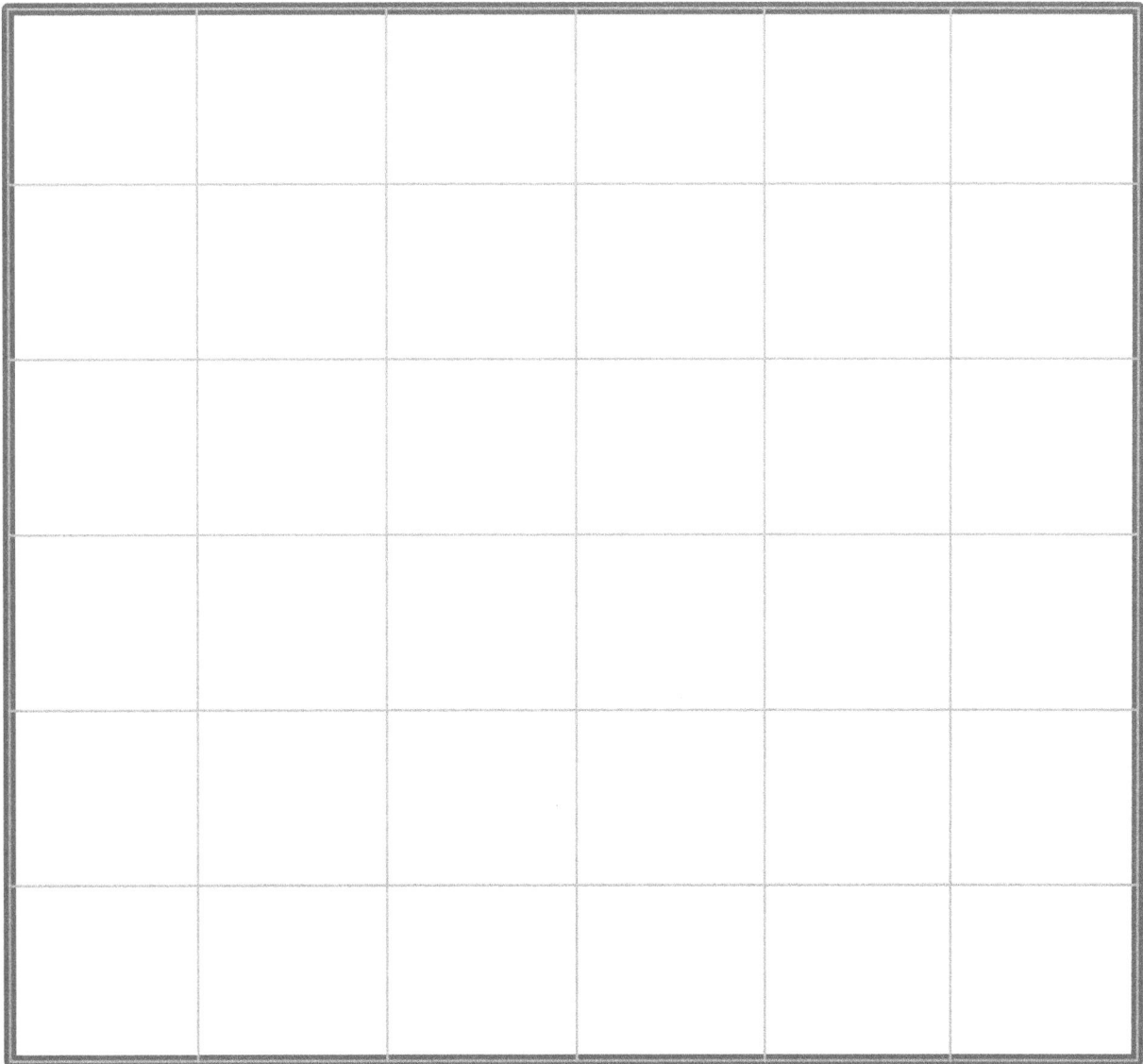

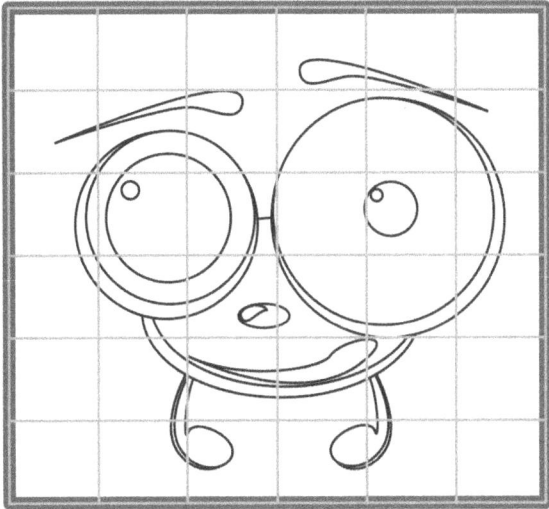

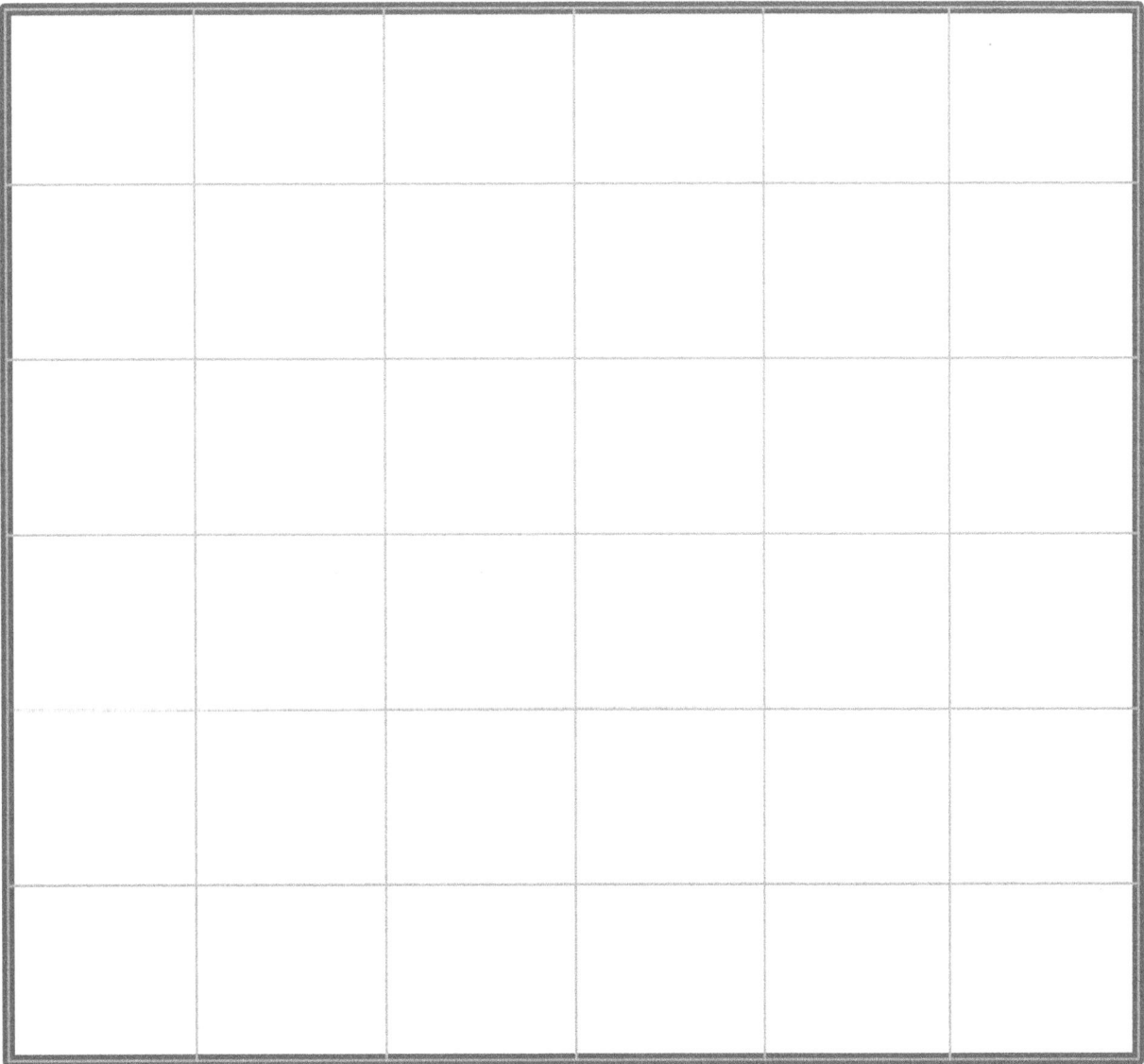

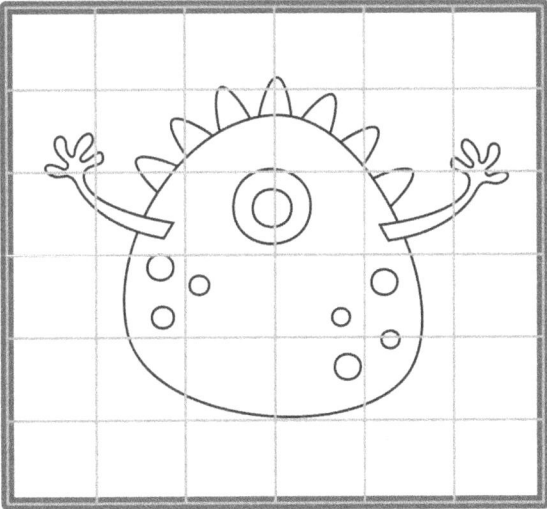

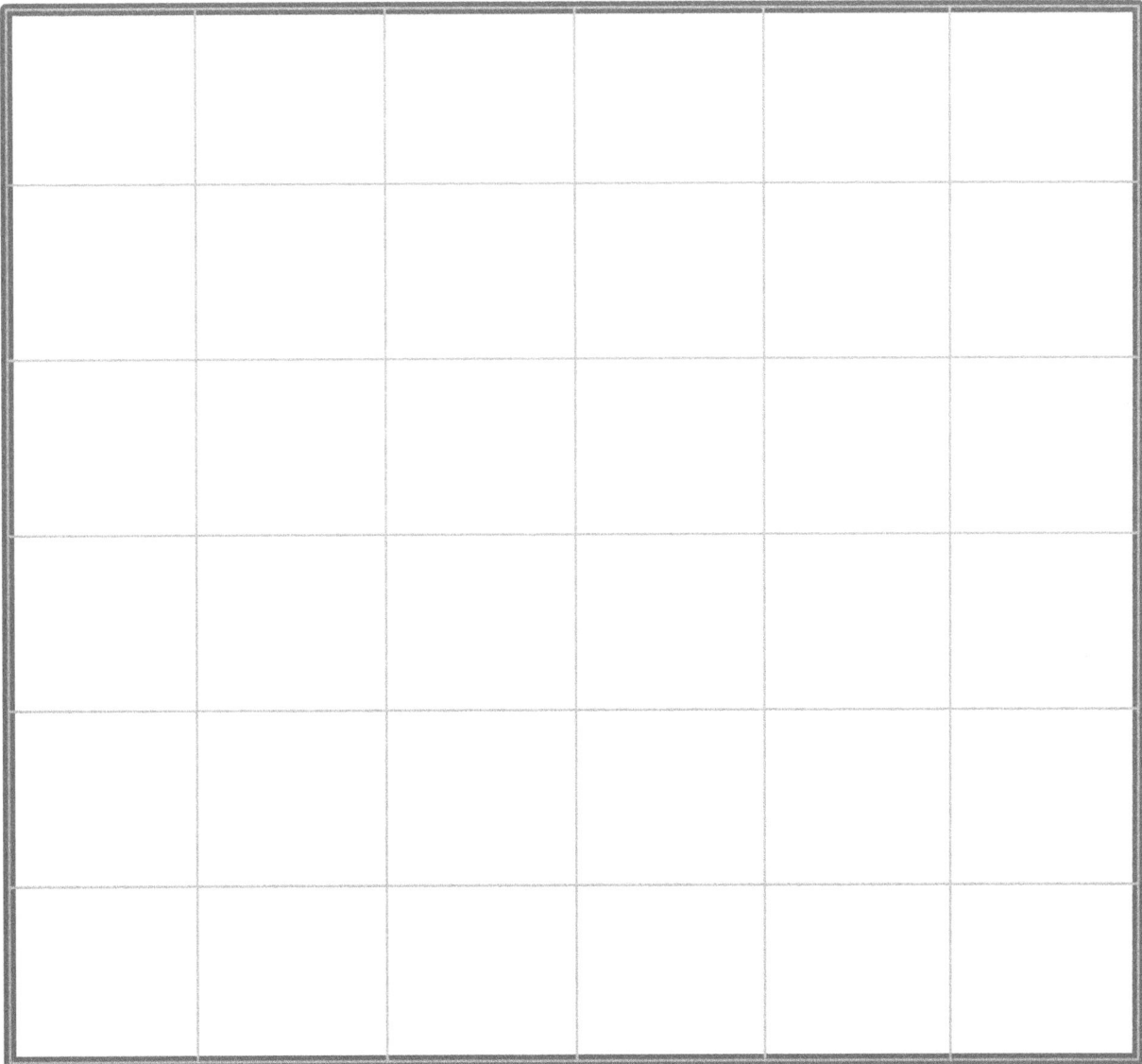

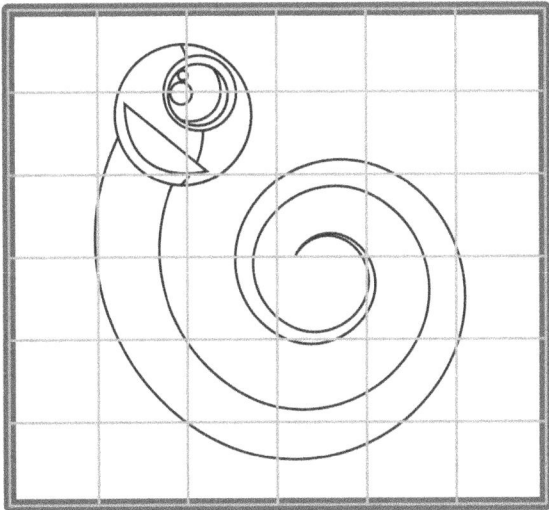

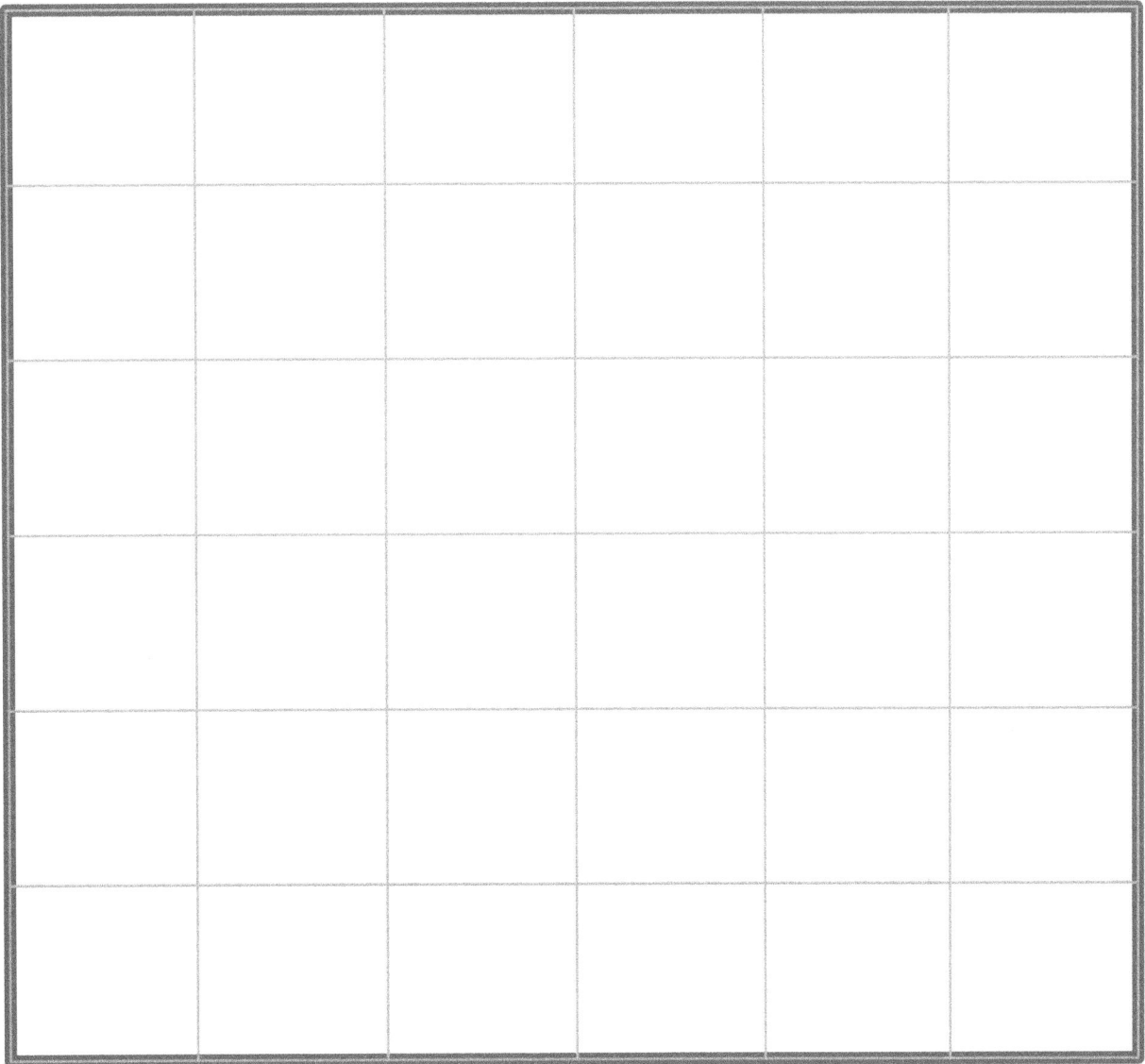

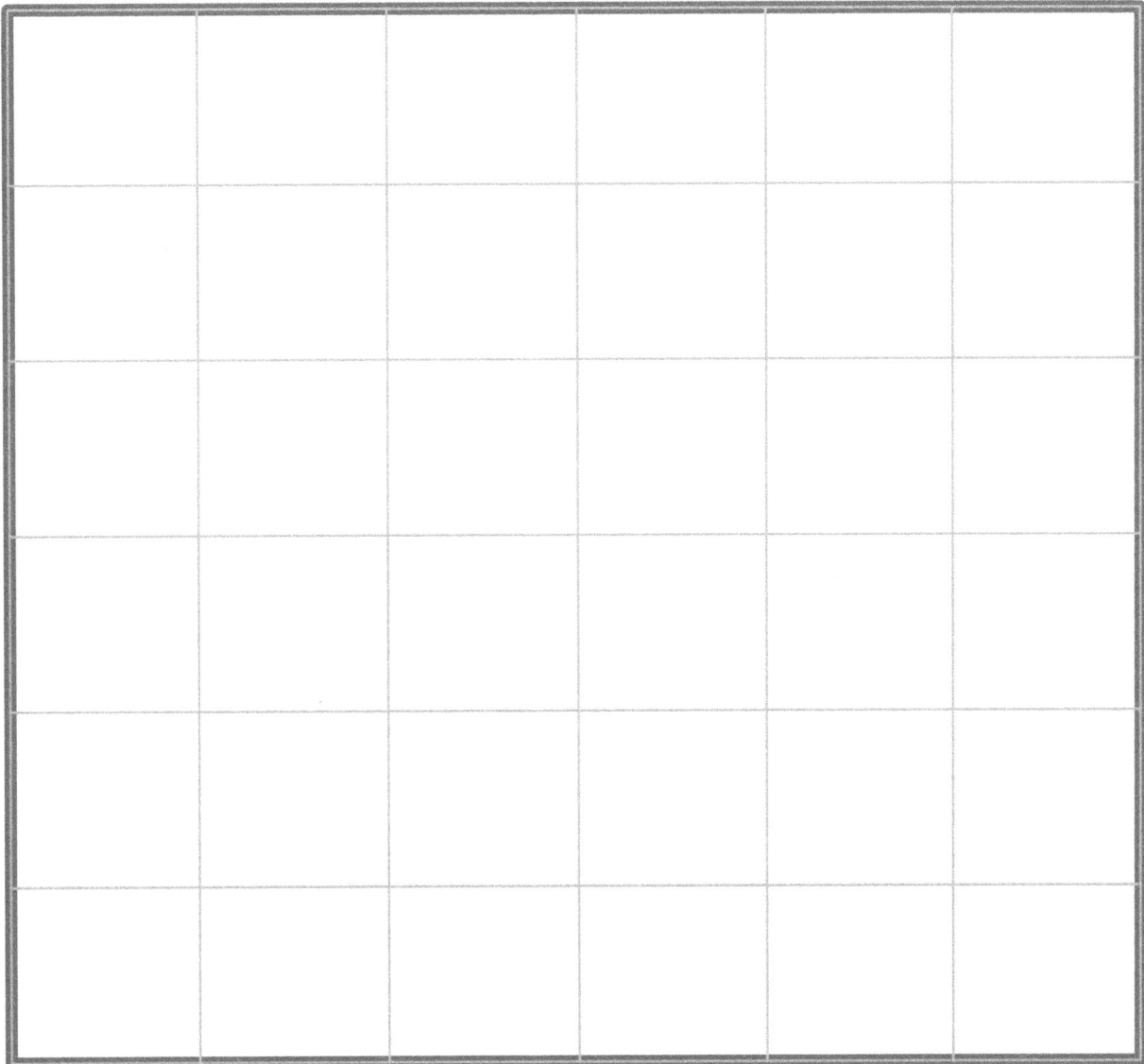

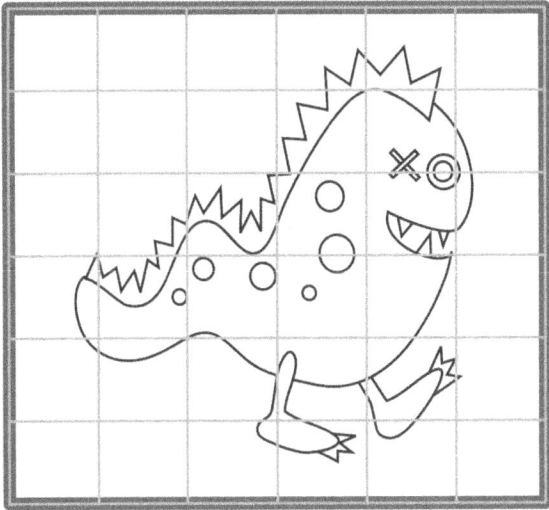

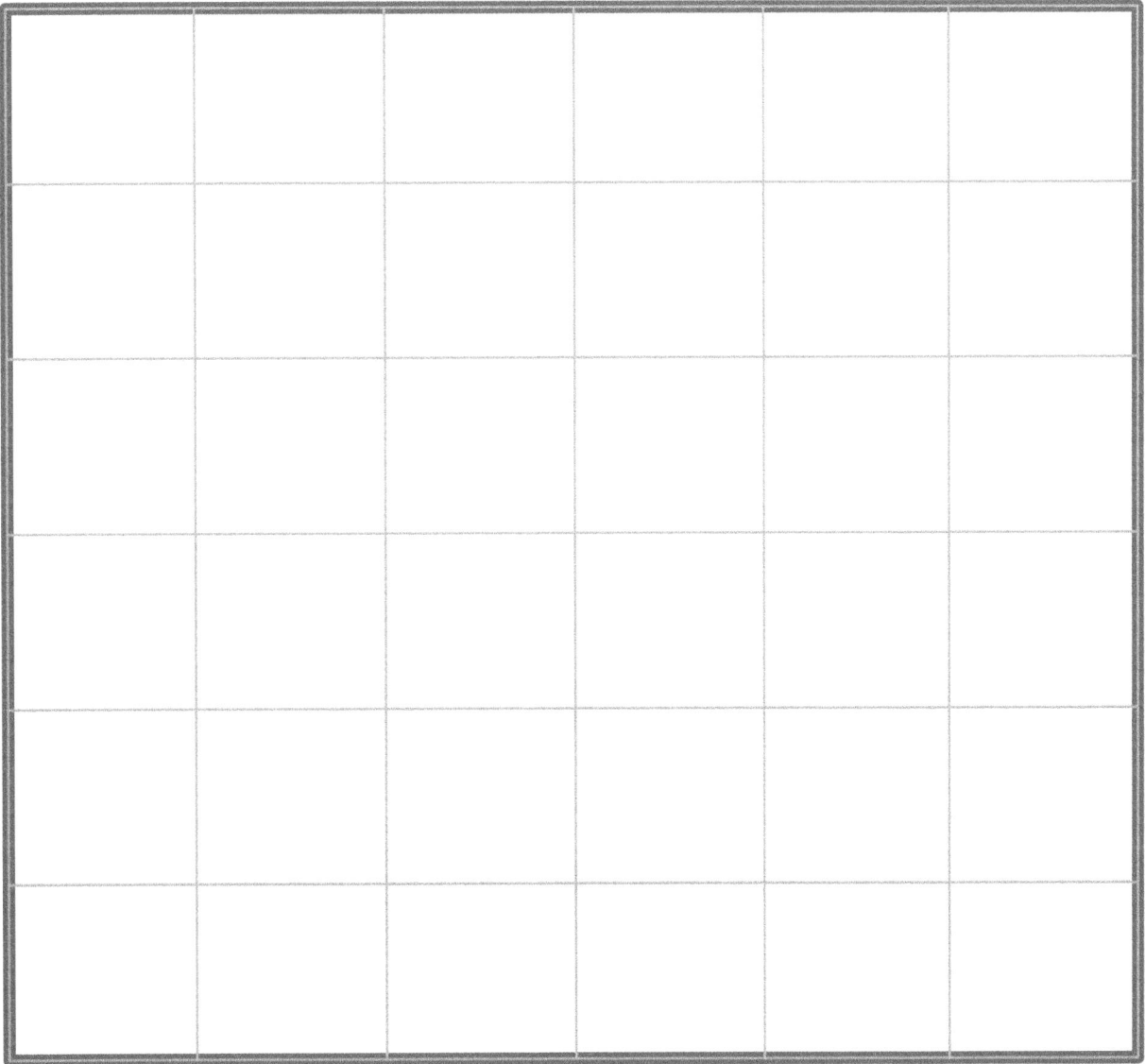

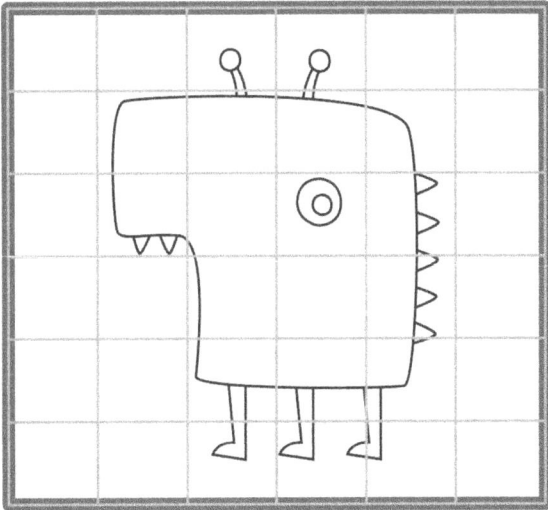

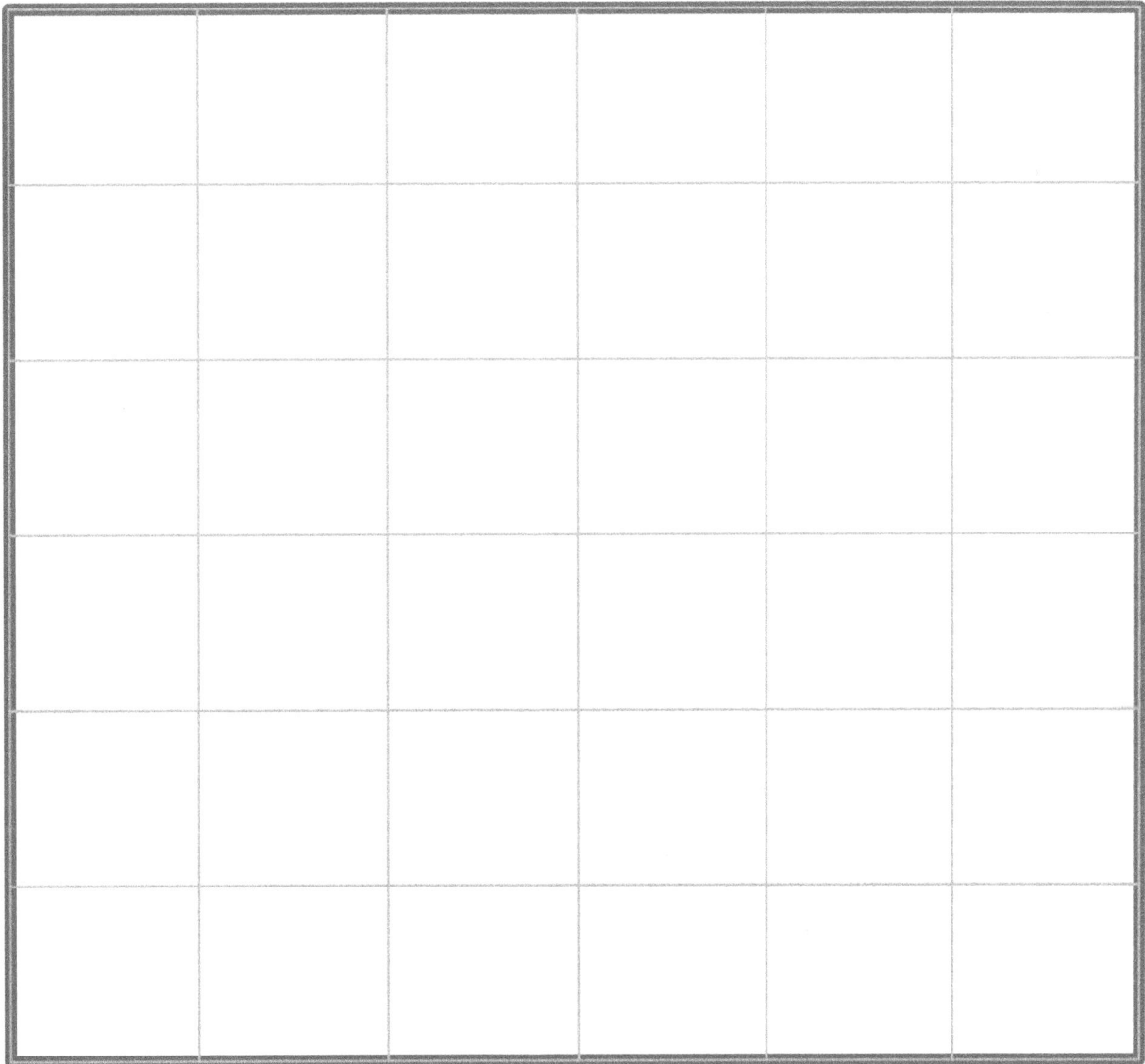

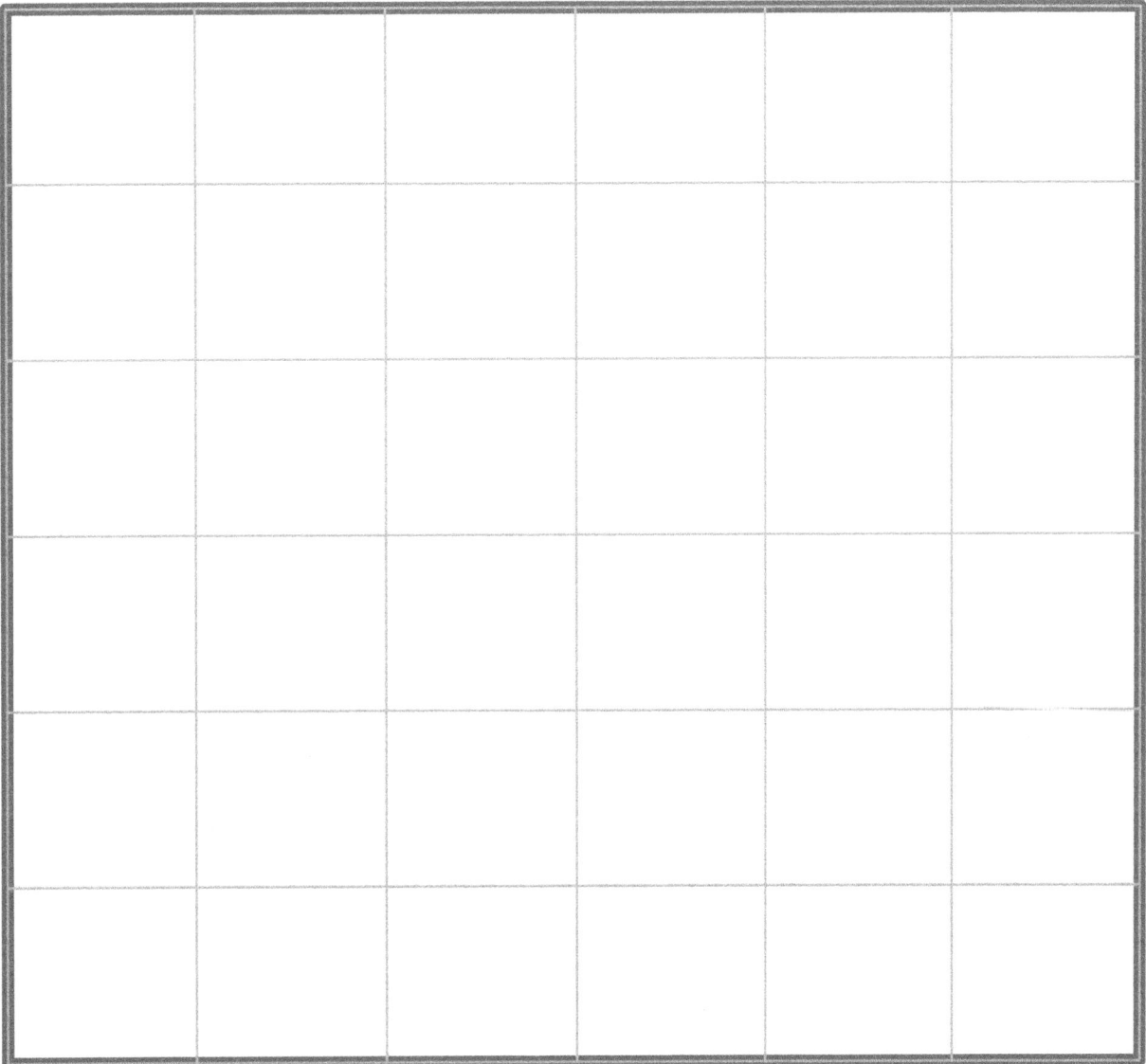

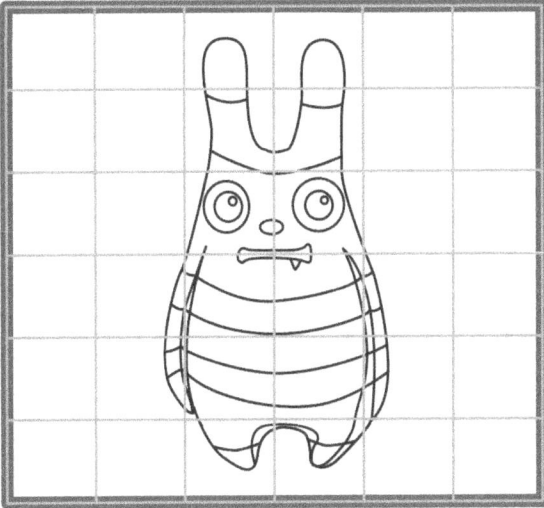

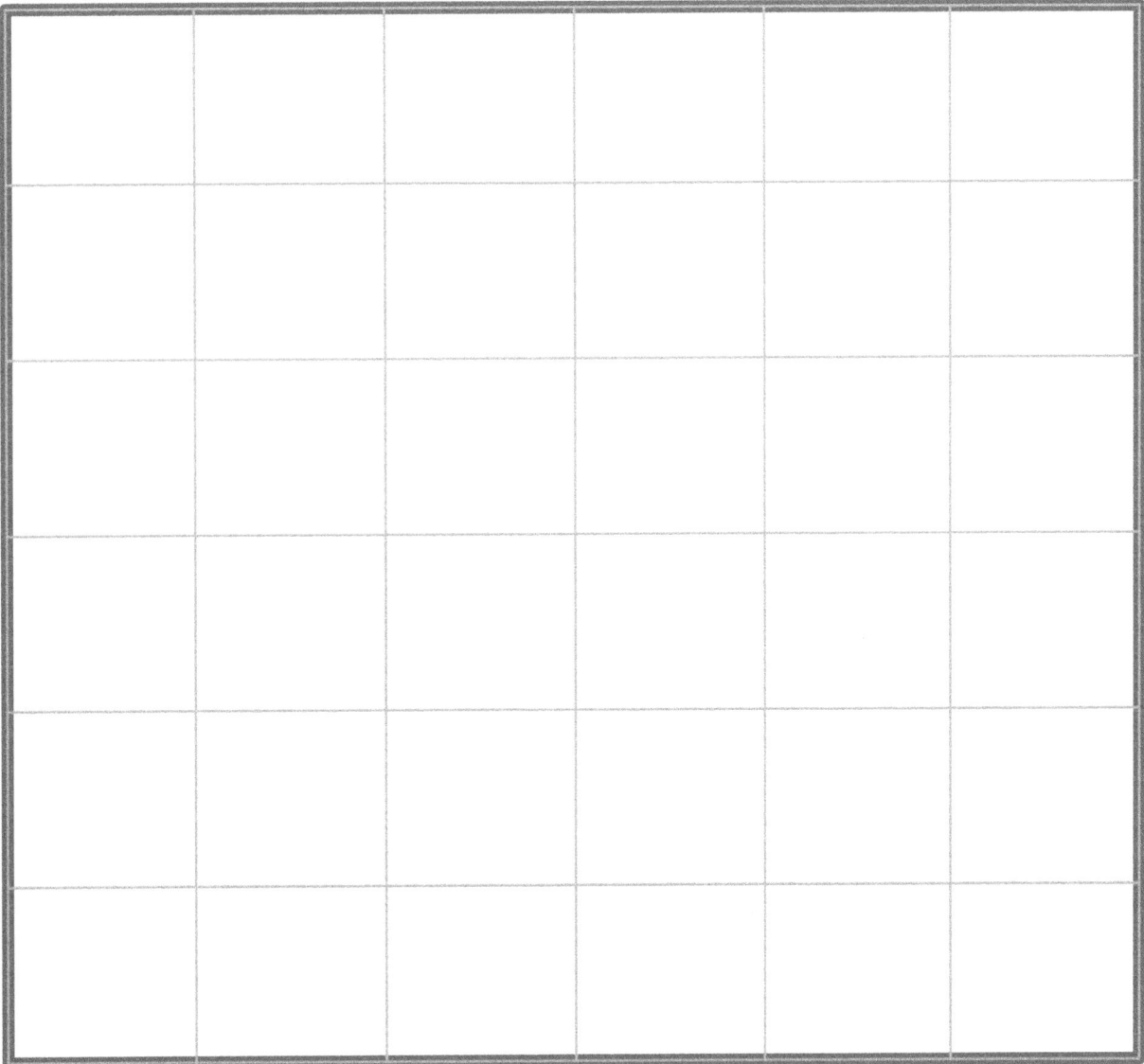

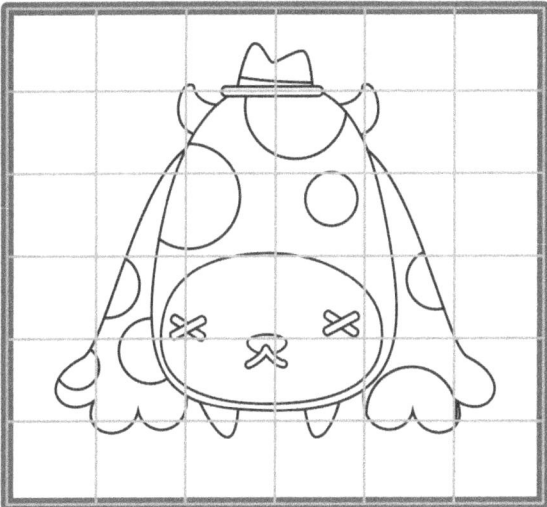

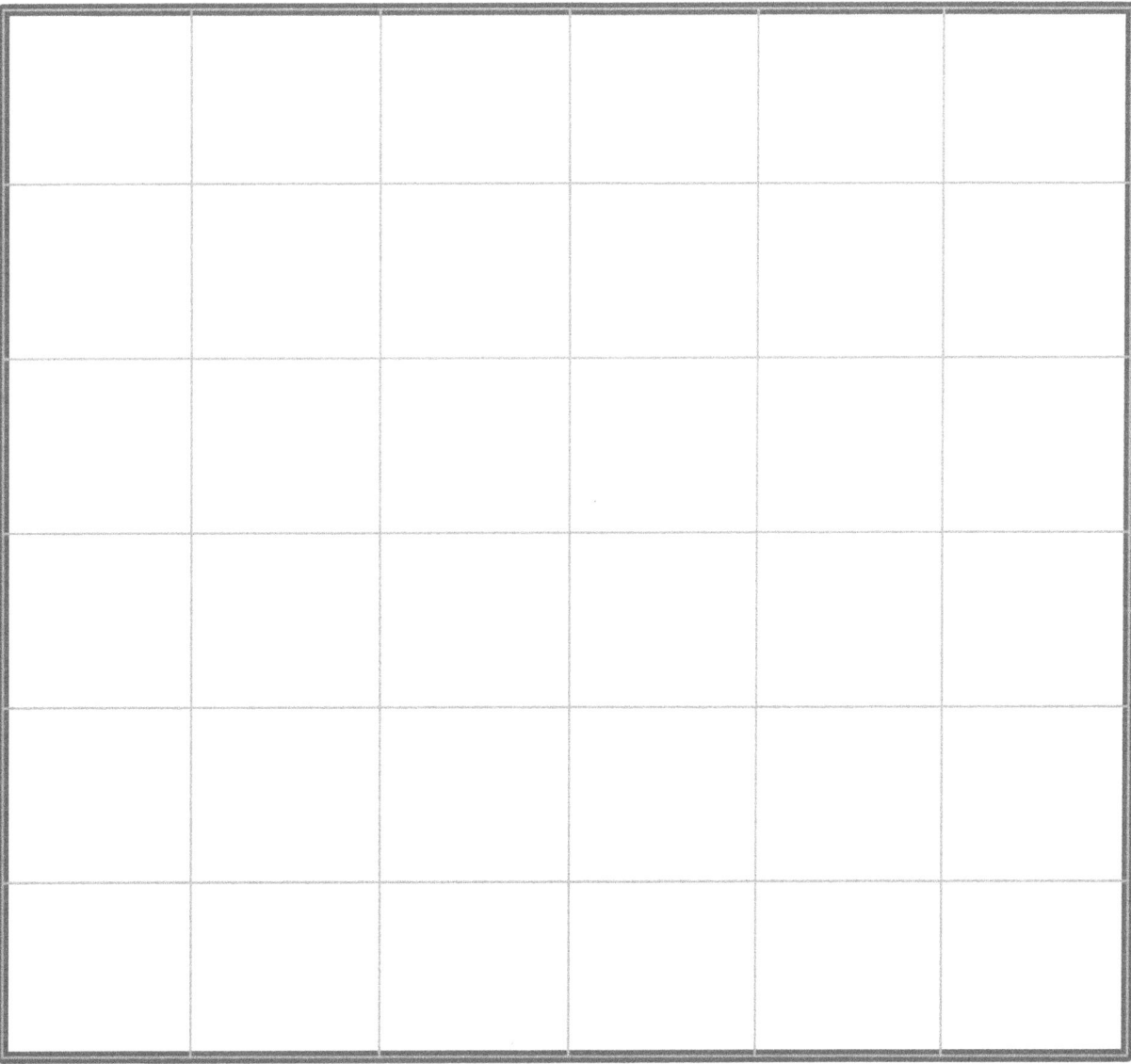

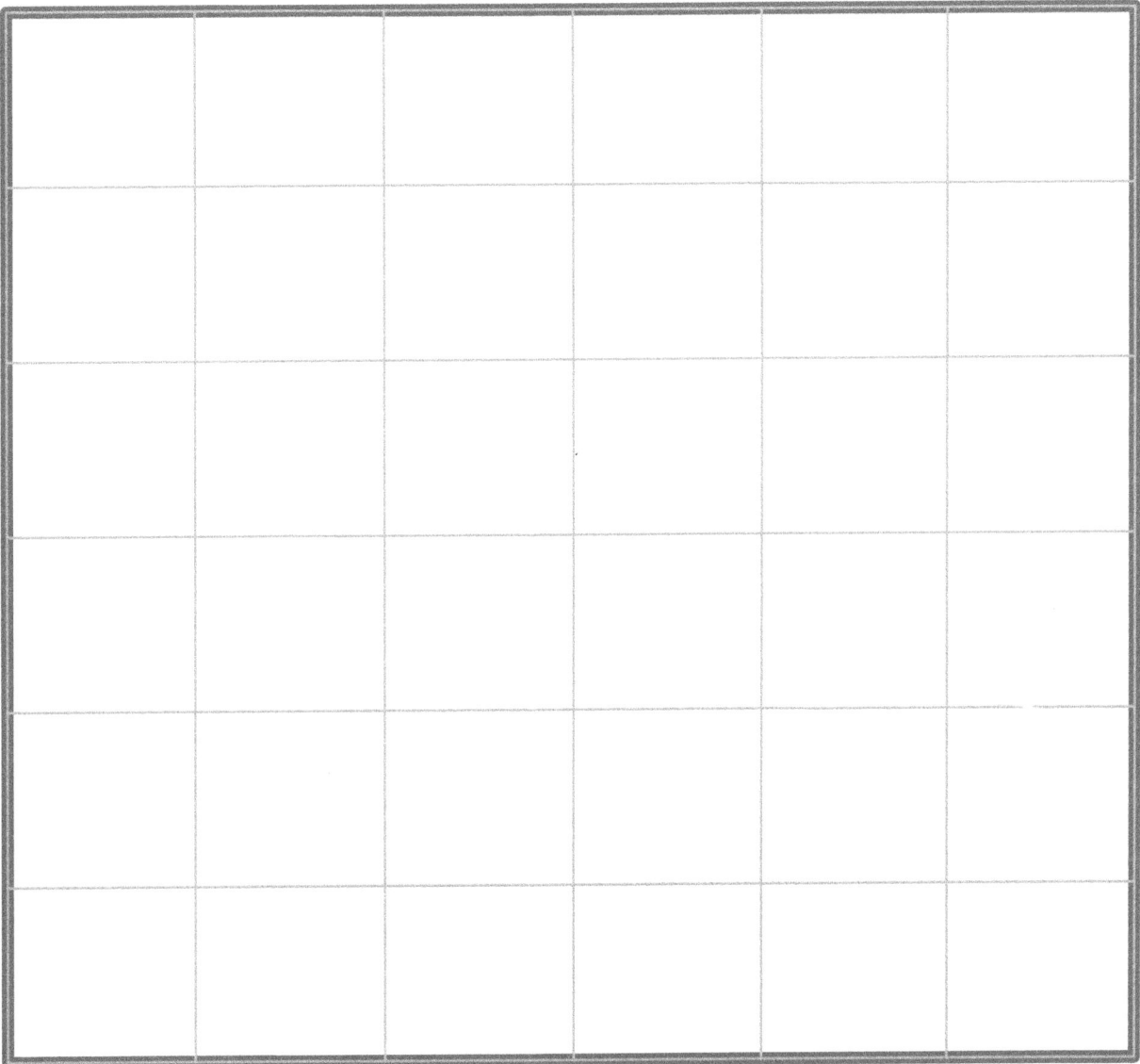

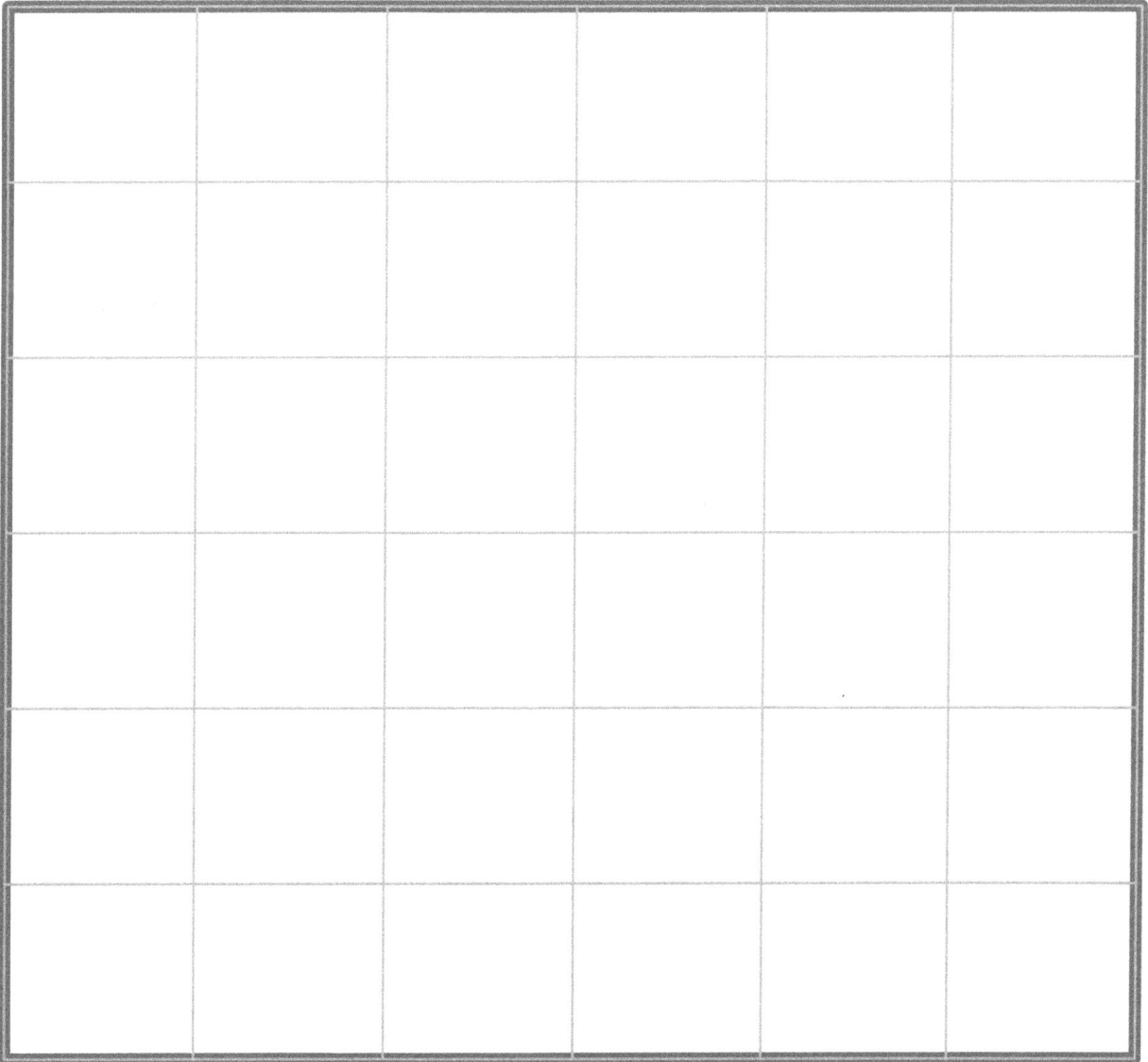

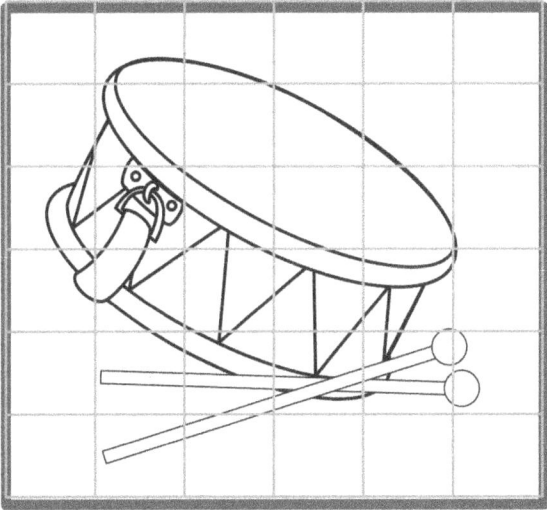

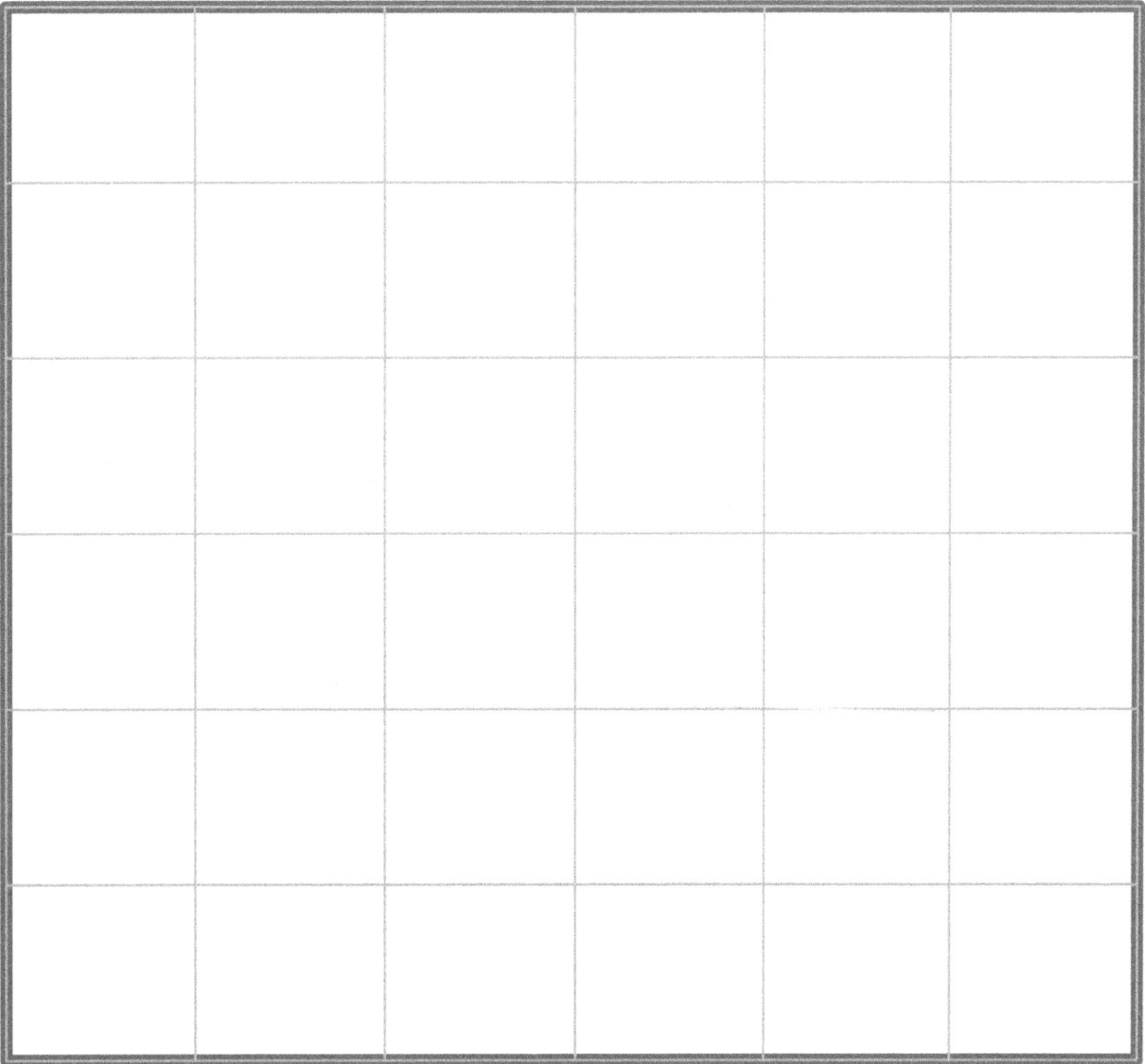

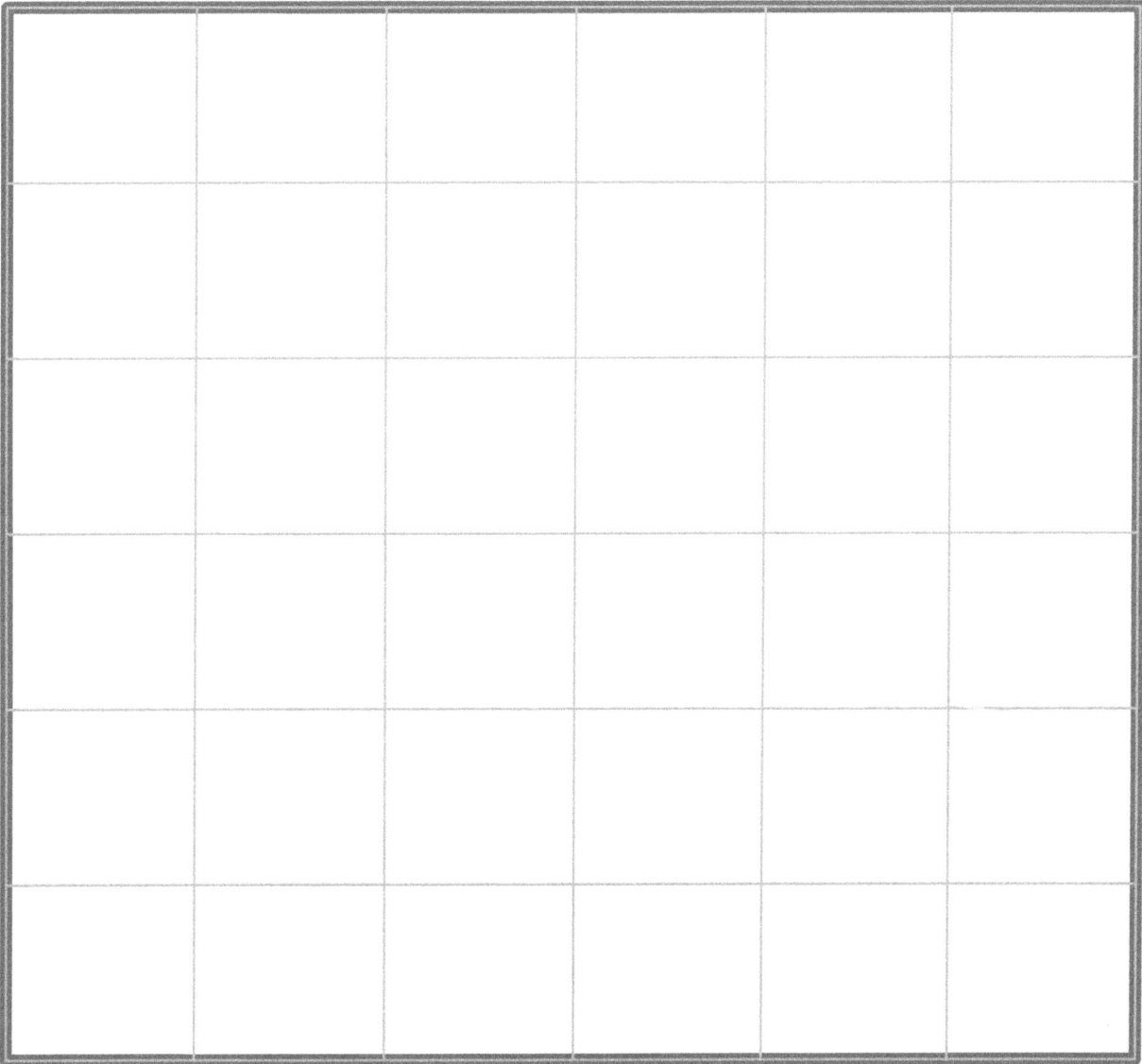

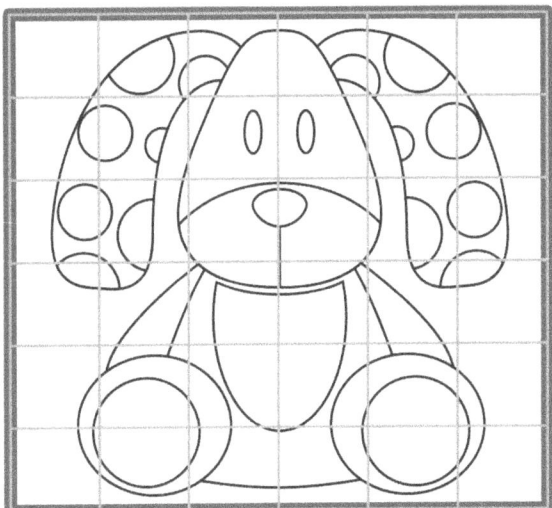

www.ingramcontent.com/pod-product-compliance
Lightning Source LLC
LaVergne TN
LVHW081334060426
835513LV00014B/1285